INCESSANT RAMBLINGS

OF A

Wilderness

Survivor

M. L. Johnston

ISBN 978-1-63961-420-2 (paperback)
ISBN 978-1-63961-421-9 (digital)

Christian Faith Publishing, Inc.
832 Park Avenue
Meadville, PA 16335
www.christianfaithpublishing.com

Printed in the United States of America

My prayer is that anyone who reads the words in this book will be set free from the captivities and strongholds in their lives. I pray God speaks to the deep seeds he has placed in your heart. I pray that each reader feels God's presence on their journey toward their promised lands. I pray God speaks deep to your broken places and heals them. I pray he opens doors to your promises. I pray each reader feels God's love and affection for them through the words on each page. I pray readers learn to cherish and embrace the wilderness' lessons, even those that are the hardest and most painfully learned. And I pray that once free, formerly enslaved kings and queens become angry about the injustices of this world. I pray readers rise up as a kingdom army and fight back in prayer and love for their brothers and sisters to expand God's kingdom. I pray for you, the reader, that you will be immensely blessed through your wilderness journey. Above all, I pray for great transformation in the deepest existence of all readers.

In Jesus's name.
Amen.

Introduction

Apartheid, it was a law that allowed South African government to segregate Whites from Blacks. If hatred was a current, apartheid was its conduit. Nelson Mandela was a man who saw the injustice that apartheid stood for as did many others. Mandela and others like him proved there was a necessity for change. He braved dangerous feats, taking drastic measures in order to see essential disruptions in government occur. Mandela was imprisoned for his anti-apartheid work.

However, Mandela not only was later released from prison, but he also became South Africa's first Black president. Mandela was *more* than a conqueror.

What injustices and even strongholds exist in your life? What captivity has you enslaved and chained to Satan's design? If your greatest wounds or strongholds were a current, what is the conduit? What if you learned to see spiritually that apartheid even slavery over our souls does exist?

Though it is unacceptable to minimize the atrocities Black Africans faced, Mandela's story points directly to the ability to overcome and exactly how radical God is. Mandela's story is one that we can all glean from. It proves that Satan may try to wreck worlds and shatter lives. Destruction may have its hour, but it is God who esteems the lowly to higher ground. Mandela's life also proves that no matter where a person is, they can become greatly separated from that enslavement beyond what our minds can remotely imagine.

I believe your life, though it may be separate in circumstances, is no different. If you're in a season of stronghold or repression, it is likely God is seeking to use your particular pit for purposes that your eyes cannot fathom.

The problem for our minds is that of vision. As God begins to reveal our purposes and his plan, the journey will feel unpleasant. Unpleasant is only a minimal representation of reality. Torturous is more accurate in describing the course.

What would Mr. Mandela tell you about his moments, hours, days, weeks, months, and years in captivity? It's unlikely he would call those moments pleasurable. But it's possible he would consider them to be formative for the Promised Land that awaited him. Similarly, when you make it to your promised land, you will find that your wilderness prepared you for the weight of your promises.

The Journey Ahead

What if the Israelites had maps? Would the trip have been shorter? What if you were enslaved, and you were given a promise by God for a land where you would be free from your captor? Then God gave you the address of the Promised Land. As you excitedly plugged your address into your navigation system, you heard, "Calculating, you will reach your destination in forty years."

Would you still be as excited about the promises of God? Would you even be interested in the Promised Land if you knew it meant you must journey into the wilderness? Would you still be excited knowing that what you want, you're going to have to fight for? Would you believe you had even heard from God if you were told during your journey, your refreshments would rain from heaven, and water would come from speaking to a rock? Or would you instead believe that what you heard was enough evidence to earn yourself a nice designer straight jacket? Would you tell anyone where it is you were going? Would you be afraid to take the first step toward the Promised Land? Would you feel that realizing your dreams was impossible? Nelson Mandela once said, "It always seems impossible until it's done." The truth is overcoming anything will feel weighty and impossible. Overcoming is, however, doable.

When God gives promises, he gives them with little detail. But if most knew the journey ahead meant having to fight to break strongholds, losing friends, broken hearts, total dependence on God, and blind faith in the wilderness, they likely wouldn't even saddle up their camels. If most saw the journey ahead and knew that it meant God would work in ways they had never seen, they may think they misunderstood the promises. When promised a new life, many would expect smooth sailing and forget that there is time and distance between our enslaved dwelling and victory.

This is likely why God chooses to give us promises with miniscule descriptions of what the journey will look like. Otherwise, it's doubtful anyone would follow his guidance toward his promises. God does, however, provide comfort for the journey. He gives provision for needs on the path. He gives strength and wisdom, but often the way he does so is by meeting each specific need during the moment it is needed, perhaps even when you think he won't come through at all.

When you've been given a promise to overcome slavery (or strongholds) of whatever flavor, be it debt, pains of the past, stepping into purposes, etc. and have been given promises toward a better future, it is exciting. At least it starts out that way.

The journey through the wilderness though isn't always what one imagines. Some may get excited by the idea of the wilderness. After all, some enjoy camping. Another idea of roughing it is not having an en suite hot tub. The wilderness can be challenging. No matter how hard the journey, God is unchanging. He will help you in the navigation of your wilderness.

The purpose of this book is to assist in the navigation from slavery of strongholds to the Promised Land of freedom and purpose. This is a map per se made to lessen the hardships of the journey. Maybe this isn't necessarily glamping, but at least this provides a good old-fashioned "wilderness survival guide." Hopefully this book will decrease the confusion on the journey and show you that just because the things you're facing are hard, it doesn't mean you're not right on track.

The greater goal is to help you realize whatever strongholds are over your life, they're not permanent. The captors of your specific enslavement may be speaking to you. Your strongholds may show you a designed purpose in God's plan for your life. God will give you promptings of how he desires to use you.

More specifically speaking, free people desire to see people set free. If you're battling one specific stronghold, you may find offense with those particular strongholds over others. This may spark your interest in going back to your "Egypt" (the battles you've overcome) to free enslaved, entrapped, and despairing people. Think of Moses, he went back to free those he saw injustices against. Someone I very much love was once a slave to his debt and financial strongholds. When I told him of my financial battles, he eagerly and with no hesitation offered, "I can help you if you want." He could only do so because he had been there and knew the way out. He had compassion for my financial strongholds because he had worn those shackles.

Esther was a queen who saved her people, but she was once an orphan. I believe Esther had such great compassion because of her humble beginnings. Orphan turned queen seems almost oxymoronic. It is the extreme circumstance that God is looking to use. I believe he sometimes says, "Plot twist," and makes the greatest stories from the biggest messes. Therefore, if you're in a mess, take heart, he has a plan.

How do you fit into the list of stories (like Esther's, Nelson Mandela's, and so many more) and plans of God's design? What is God getting ready to do in and through you? Could it be that you have been designed for "such a time as this?" Is it possible that the chains you feel over your life are pointing in the direction of your purpose?

Saddle up. Let's take this journey.

Chapter 1

Leaving Egypt
The Fight for Freedom

It's feasible that social norms will always elude me. Or perhaps I simply forgot the first rule of fight club. But somebody has to bring it up. Someone has to talk about the fight required for freedom. Should that mean that I will be found in a dark alley? I'm willing to risk it. Otherwise, some will never realize their dreams.

Therefore, I'll take my chances. I'll talk about the fight. That is the fight required to make it to the Promised Land. If you want freedom from strongholds, freedom from captivity, if you want to walk in your promises, you must fight for freedom. You must fight for what you want. And that fight begins against an enslaved mentality. Spiritual fight club is real. And the second you picked up this book, you became a member.

Enslaved Mentality

John Brown was an abolitionist. He had the perfect combination of a desire to free slaves paired with a bit of testosterone-saturated recklessness. John considered himself to be the Moses of his time. He was passionate about his cause. Even if it meant laying down his life, Brown had every intention of seeing captives set free.

Determined to arm slaves with necessary weapons to break them free from their captors, Mr. Brown assembled an army. With his crew and a considerable dosage of passion-laced insanity, Brown broke into the national armory to obtain weaponry so that slaves could finally fight back and become free.

Brown was, however, unaware of one problem; the slaves had been conditioned to believe they had no ability to fight back. Once Brown gave the slaves their tools for battle, he quickly found his efforts were in vain. The slaves would not use what they had been given for freedom. Mr. Brown tragically was hanged for treason.

Why though? How is it that these people were given weapons for warfare yet were so afraid? Surely if they fought, they would win. One slave owner versus a crew of slaves armed for battle would lose. The slaves weren't aware of what we know now that freedom was on the other side of a battle. They had likely seen what happened to other slaves who didn't conform. They possibly witnessed the lynching of loved ones. They had a home. It may not be what they wanted, but if they became free, where would they go? They had food. It may cost sweat, blood, tears, and broken spirits, but they were comfortable with their enemy. Slaves were much like broken elephants.

When elephants are taken captive by those who intend to use them for entertainment purposes, they are broken. It is called "elephant crushing." The elephants are abused into submission. They're placed into tiny confines with no room to move. The elephants are then poked with sticks in their ears and further abused until the spirit of the elephant gives in. They're beaten by abusers, chained, starved (more on how starvation pertains to you in chapter 2). They're crushed. This causes the elephant to no longer fight. Once the elephant loses its desire to resist control, it is officially broken. An elephant, a majestic and mighty creature, with no fight is a heartbreaking sight. As is any captive who won't fight back.

From mighty elephants to tiny ants? There is no way to segue this paragraph; therefore, I dare not try. Dear beloved reader, follow my squirrel trails, and together we will find the point. When ants find hummingbird food, they will often help themselves to the buffet of sugary delight. In my younger years, my dad had gotten tired of seeing ants in his bird feeders. Therefore, he made chalk lines around the edge of the feeder hanger. Ants will not cross chalk lines. So as a bit of a mean-spirited person I once was and am now reformed from, I decided to draw circles around ants to see if they would stay within the confines of the lines. They did.

Is it possible that you've had lines of chalk drawn around your spirit to keep you confined? Is it possible that like broken elephants in your broken hours, Satan has been crushing your spirit? Are you like the majestic elephant, mighty but afraid of the fight? Are you like the slaves of John Brown's day? Afraid to take shots even if you know your freedom and purpose is on the other side of the battle?

God wants his children to be free. The unfortunate truth is that there is an enemy of souls that has waged war against your freedom, against your purpose. Satan has vested interest in keeping you captive. If your soul is afraid to fight, he can keep one or potentially many from ever making it to freedom. This is about the kingdom, not you. If you're free, you will (hopefully) empower other slaves and break them free. So Satan wages war against your spirit in hopes you will be like broken elephants, mighty but without a drive to fight. He wants you like ants with lines of chalk around you to keep you confined by ridiculous borders. He wants you like the slaves of Brown's day, too afraid to fight, too afraid to wage war against him, and too afraid to win as God has designed you to do.

Satan is like Pharaoh in Exodus 1:8–14. He sees the nation of God's children becoming great. Similar to pharaoh who saw the Israelites increased in number, Satan sees your strength, and it scares your enemy. As pharaoh became afraid of the Israelites and their power in numbers, afraid they would take over, Pharaoh became a slave driver to his people. Similarly, Satan sees your power, so he is determined to keep you enslaved.

If Satan can keep people distracted and enslaved to their financial problems, family history, brokenness, depression, strongholds, historical mistakes, the enemy feels he has won. That's because a person cannot be both, free and enslaved. You cannot be a slave and a queen. Once a person begins to understand their identity, they are no longer willing to remain as slaves. What Satan is banking on is the belief that we won't read the rest of the story or fight back. However, the rest of the story says slaves break free. Use this information to fight, to become free, and to walk in purposeful victory.

You, sweet sister or brother, are children of the Most High King of kings. You are royals. And royals were never purposed for slavery. If you have a Bible and the ability to pray, you're armed. It's time to fight back. It's time to erase the chalk lines around your life. It is time to recognize you're a majestic creature more powerful than you realize. It's time to become free. It's time to journey to the Promised Land. It's time to become kings and queens living in purpose.

You have been armed. Your weapons are scriptures, prayers, and proclamation of victory. The question is, "Will you be like the slaves of Brown's day, refusing to fight back, or will you take the shots?"

Wayne Gretzky said it best, "You will miss 100 percent of the shots you don't take." And you can't win a war if you're unwilling to go to a battle. So if you're armed, why won't you fight? Why are Christians not taking their rightful places as kingdom heirs?

Why? Because too many are unaware of their power. They have been fighting what they see as a losing battle. Like the slaves of Brown's era, broken people stay broken, unaware they have a fighting chance at becoming free. Many calculate debt, personal history, shame, etc. into the equation of their battle. That's because they're listening to the voice of the enemy. Like any slave master, Satan knows he cannot win the battle against you, so he will convince you that your obstacles are bigger than you. He wants to keep you from fighting back, so he fills your heart, mind, and soul with lies. He will very strategically wage war against your determination. He will keep lies ringing in your ears. "You've tried and failed before. A person like you has no chance of overcoming your past. Your dreams seem great, but they are unattainable. You're too old to accomplish the dream. Getting out of debt and reaching financial freedom sounds lovely, but your obstacles are too big. Your family are nothing but a bunch of redneck losers. There is no way to overcome a name such as yours. That dream God put in your heart, if only, you don't stand a chance. The things you want are only for others."

It's time to change this mentality. Stop believing the lies. Stop allowing Satan's devices to become greater than your belief.

Satan is like a yappy Chihuahua in comparison to a Great Dane. The Chihuahua may bark all day, but if the Great Dane chose to, it could eat the Chihuahua for breakfast. Satan knows that if you choose to bite back, you will win. Satan uses a lot of scare tactics against you. But in reality, he is yappy, annoying, and powerless against the power of God within you. (Greater is he living in you than he who is in the world.)

Use What You Have

My middle child was bullied when he was a young lass. I don't necessarily remember the circumstances, but I do remember one particular thing standing out to me. He was an absolute brute in his karate classes. He was often told to hold back a little by his instructor because he could really put a hurtin' on other classmates if he didn't. Yet day in and day out, I had a young child who hated going to school because of his fear of another boy.

I would often think, *How is it he's such a force in one area but terrified in another?* The answer lies in the fact that one area of his life wasn't applied to another. He didn't even have to use his karate skills on the bully. But he needed to remember what he knew about his strength, and I doubt he would have had any fear.

Why is it that we have knowledge yet never apply it? Why is it that in the classroom of life, we're given lessons of sheer brutality that when unleashed would conquer mountains, yet we tremble in fear? That is passivity at its finest. That is the price of choosing not to fight. The toll is loss, and it is a cost you must decide you're unwilling to pay.

"Fighting" requires faith-filled courage, and courage filled action. If you want to be free, you cannot be like the passive slaves of John Brown's era. If you want to be free, you must first recognize you have a John Brown, a "Moses." You have Jesus who broke into the armory of the spiritual and unseen to obtain weapons for spiritual warfare. He fought on the cross and was tragically hung with the price of our lives on the line. Will you allow it to be in vain?

Cooter Brown

What if? What if you chose not to fight? Is that the legacy you want to leave? A legacy of unwillingness to participate? You were created with purpose. But it takes faith and action to fulfill destiny. It takes fighting against the voices that tell you that you're not good enough to win. But what if you chose not to fight back?

Let me paint a picture for you, the one who chooses not to fight. I'll call you Cooter Brown. Why? We have all heard of him, the one whose name is dropped the minute someone participated a little too heavily in recreational boozing. "He's drunker than Cooter Brown." We've heard the idiom, but where did it come from?

Cooter Brown was an American man who was said to have had family members on either side of the civil war battle. He was afraid to fight for either side knowing his family may become the people he was fighting against. He understandably didn't want to participate in wartime activities. He was uninterested to say the least, so he came up with a plan to avoid all chances of being drafted by either party. He chose to become so drunk that he was useless to both union and confederate troops.

The sad truth, after the war, Cooter was said to have become an alcoholic. Who of us couldn't identify with Brown and feel sympathetic toward his conundrum? It's hard to villainize Brown when we're aware that his burden was so great. I do, however, question what would have happened if he chose to fight on his knees instead of taking matters into his own hands. Or more accurately speaking, what would have happened if he had not been so passive and chose to wage war against an enemy who said slaves must remain slaves. Would we know the name Cooter Brown to be that of a pickled liver? If he fought, would we have known his name to be a household hero who led others to freedom? Avoiding war left Brown to struggle with unforeseen battles that he lost that is the enslaved life of alcoholism.

Very few want to fight their loved ones. However, when it comes to spiritual warfare, the cost of not participating in the battle is far greater than most of us want to pay. Unfortunately, the tragic cost of avoidance is continued enslavement or added slavery.

The first step to becoming free from Satan's enslaved, entrapped plan for your life is to become determined that you're sick of living as he has designed. You must refuse to stay in a sick place, expecting to obtain the promises of God. His Promised Land isn't laced with tainted poisonous fruit of passivity. And the Promised Land is not ruled by Pharaoh or any slave master of Satan's design. You must become certain that you can fight, you can win, and the cost of not doing so is one you're unwilling to pay.

Furthermore, you have to gain enough strength to recognize that even though you've been enslaved to anything doesn't mean that thing or slavery period is due to a false identity. Your attacks are directly proportional to your identity, more specifically speaking... your purpose. The greater the attack, the larger the plan God has for your life. You must get that deep into your spirit. Please become armed with the knowledge of God and his love for you that Satan knows you're not the one he wants to mess with.

When he barks, bite back. When he tells you you can't win, remind him of his fate and of yours. Remind him whose child you are and of his imminent end. When Satan says you can't, proclaim that God said you can. God is not a man that he should lie. When Satan reminds you of your failure, remind him of the mistake he made by betraying God. When he reminds you of your shortcomings, simply say, "That's okay. I can't, but God can. And with him, I will." You must take every shot toward victory.

Frontline Warriors

Many Christians have their biblical favorites. If you were given the opportunity to have dinner with just one, aside from the obvious, Jesus, who would you choose? My suspicion is that the minute you read that last sentence, a name flashed in your mind. Myself? I've always wished I could meet Job, Ruth, and one unsung hero, Uriah.

Uriah, in summary, was a man betrayed not only by his friend and king but also by his beloved bride. While Uriah was at war, David had an affair with his wife. (The wife that the Bible makes strong mention of Uriah's love and devotion to.) When King David found he had impregnated Uriah's wife, he offered Uriah the opportunity to come home to his bride. David hoped to frame Uriah for the pregnancy to avoid accountability. Unfortunately for David, Uriah refused to deny his patriotic duties. He chose to stay in war. Because of this, David had Uriah sent to the frontline to have him killed.

As a hopeless romantic, I have always admired Uriah. His story fostered belief that one man could truly love his "one and only lamb" to the deepest parts of his core. Uriah seemingly was the type of man who was noble and honorable. He was ready to fight for his kingdom even when given the chance to come home to his beloved wife. Uriah seemed to be the ideal form of what a man "should be."

However, there is this part of me that always wondered, *Was it God protecting his heart? Did God allow Uriah's frontline misfortune so that Uriah would never know the pain of his wife's affair?* I somehow believe Uriah had the better outcome of never knowing his beloved had betrayed him.

More recently, I have questioned the details of this storyline on a deeper level. Did Uriah know more than he ever admitted? After all, a passive person who has been cheated on often knows more than they show. Sometimes betrayal not acknowledged is left unspoken out of heartache. Their hearts cannot confront the pain. So I question, "Did Uriah know? Did he choose to go back to war knowing the wounds he faced at home were far greater than any wounds war could ever inflict?"

No matter the details, all of us could stand to learn from our biblical brother Uriah. He was betrayed; he fought anyway. His heart was attached to a love that could have kept him home. He chose war.

All of us have the details of our lives that others could only speculate about. Most will never know the heartaches and betrayals you've faced. Fight anyway. It's doubtful others would understand what it cost for you to fight. Regardless you must choose to wage war against the enemy of your soul. As Uriah was, you're standing at the gates of opportunity. Will you choose the passive way out? Or will you choose the frontline, even if it hurts? I do hope you chose war. I pray you chose to fight for whatever it is you're wanting to obtain.

Put on Your Lipstick and Man Your Guns, This Means War

My favorite video of my youngest son is of him holding a keychain with a toy gun and ChapStick on it. In the video, he is around four years old, and he is "soooting" me.

He looked at me when I didn't originally know what he was doing and said, "I sooted you, so you die."

After he finished, he stopped and nonchalantly applied his ChapStick as if to say, "I win, and I'm going to walk forward in victory."

This is what I'm asking of you as you begin walking on your path to freedom. I ask that you shoot, that you fight. When Satan doesn't get it, make sure he understands your shots are for his demise. Take back the design and purpose for your life. Fight Satan, and when you get done taking each shot, you apply your lipstick (or ChapStick) and walk in victory. No matter the cost, fight and become free.

Above all, when your mind says, "I can't." Remember, God's word says, "With me, you can." And that's the only words you need to know.

Lower the Gates

Call me petty if you will. That's fine. One of my greatest frustrations with one of my employers, past, present, or future (okay, hopefully not future) is that of parking. Day in and day out, I have arrived to work to find no parking in the employee parking lot.

Don't get me wrong; it isn't that I'm entitled to a personal golden parking space with my name on it. Entitlement isn't the case at all. The problem is that the employee parking lot is gated. Yet the gates entering the lot are always open for the entire city and surrounding areas.

Employee parking lots are not churches; therefore, all who enter are not welcomed. The employees of this particular company have useless badges to open a gate that is never closed. Therefore, employees have to park significantly further away and ride a shuttle into work, and they're often late due to this fact. If this company never planned to use the gates, they could have handed out a raise or two in lieu of employee frustration.

The thing is, those who shouldn't be there often are. The solution is very simple, but despite employees voicing their frustrations, this gate is never addressed. A gate that is never used is worthless.

When it comes to spiritual warfare, you're going to have to learn how to close the gates to your mind. Not all thoughts that enter belong. Some thoughts of defeat will try to enter. Satan is always looking for a way in. So you've been fighting this battle over your future, your life of purpose, and your position in God's kingdom. Don't you think that is worth protecting? Put on the whole armor of God. Lower the gate.

Focus Scriptures and Quotes
(Weaponry)

No weapon forged against you will prevail, and you will refute every tongue that accuses you. This is the heritage of the servants of the Lord and this is the vindication from me," declares the LORD. (Isaiah 54:17 NIV)

The thief comes only to kill steal and destroy; I came so that they may have life, and have it to the full. (John 10:10 NIV)

"For I know the plans I have for you," declares the Lord, "plans to prosper you and not to harm you, plans to give you hope and a future." (Jeremiah 29:11 NIV)

I can do all things through him who gives me strength. (Philippians 4:13 NIV)

Finally, be strong in the Lord and in his mighty power. Put on the full armor of God, so that you can take your stand against the devil's schemes. For our struggle is not against flesh and blood, but against the rulers, against the authorities, against the powers of this dark world and against the spiritual forces of evil in the heavenly realms. Therefore, put on the full armor of God, so that when the day of evil comes, you may be able to stand your ground, and after you have done everything, to stand. Stand firm then, with the belt of truth buckled around your waist, with the breastplate of righteousness in place, and with your feet fitted with the readiness that comes from the gospel of peace. In addition to all this, take up the shield of faith, with which you can extinguish all the flaming arrows of the evil one. Take the helmet of salvation and the sword of the Spirit, which is the word of God. And pray in the Spirit on all occasions with all kinds of prayers and requests. With this in mind, be alert and always keep on praying for all the Lord's people. (Ephesians 6:10–18 NIV)

Death and life are in the power of the tongue: and they that love it shall eat the fruit thereof. (Proverbs 18:21 KJV)

You may have to fight a battle more than once to win it. (Margaret Thatcher)

Chapter 2

Identity Crisis

Starvation is a war tactic that has been used by tyrant leaders over many decades. Nazi Germany starved Jews and other citizens to prevent them from having strength to fight back. It's more common than most are aware and is happening in modern-day warfare. When one is starved, food becomes all they will think about. If you were so famished, your only focus is survival. Would you focus energy on fighting back?

Starvation can often lead to a condition called pica. Pica can occur from nutritional deficiencies. A person who has pica will crave nonfood items like dirt, clay, chalk, etc.

What if your enemy starved you to prevent you from having energy to fight him? What if your starvation was of the knowledge of who you are, of your worth, and of who your father is?

If you're busy trying to satisfy the cries of hunger pains, it's possible, well likely, you won't focus your energy on getting well and fighting for freedom. Furthermore, a starved soul much like someone with pica will find ways to satisfy hunger with things that aren't nutritious or beneficial to its well-being. Unfortunately, a hungry soul may barter their birthrights from desperation.

In Genesis 25:19–34, Jacob tricked Esau out of his birthright using a bowl of soup. For Esau, his hunger was more important to satisfy momentarily than keeping what was rightfully his.

If Satan keeps you hungry, he has room to trick you out of your birthrights as a child of God. Therefore, it is critical that you learn who you are and stay full of your knowledge of identity and worth. Satan will never have a chance to rob your soul of its birthright if he has nothing you're willing to bargain for.

Many options exist to feed a hungry soul. We have more distractions in this world than I could ever account for. However, not all things we're offered are worth consuming. Some distractions will leave you satisfied for a brief moment but starving soon after. A friend of mine once pointed out that she didn't like having breakfast like what we had eaten as it leads to hunger soon after. We had eaten waffles with her parents. If we had a more nutritious meal as we had consumed the rest of the weekend, we would have been satisfied much longer. We would have felt less tired and more energetic as well.

In this chapter, we will begin feeding your identity so that you will have the strength to fight for your freedom, step into your promises, and refuse to allow anything in your life that isn't good for your well-being.

I want to ask that as you recognize your identity, you will begin to pray about what is starving your soul. What distractions have you fed briefly yet left you hungry soon after? What dirt are you feeding yourself that is of no nutritional value at all? Do you feed yourself defeated thoughts? Are you consuming thoughts of failure? What do you feed yourself that renders you without energy and exhausted?

Blinded

It is important that you avoid starvation, but you also have to be careful about the nutritional components of your spiritual "diet." In September of two thousand and nineteen, a teen boy made international headlines. The teen became blind after eating a diet of only unhealthy foods.

His diet consisted of Pringles, fries, and white bread. Due to nutritional deficiencies, the teen had optic nerve damage that led to permanent blindness. Our spirits are no different. If we consume things that lack emotional value, we become blind to the truths about ourselves.

The only thing worth consuming is what God says about you. And the best way to feed that is by staying in his word and in your prayer life and relationship with him. However, I do hope this next chapter will be a satisfying snack that builds your cravings of knowledge of identity. I pray you become hungrier for your purpose and closer to your father so that you will be truly satisfied and energetic enough to walk in victory. I pray you become so full of God's truths about you that you're unwilling to digest anything less. Mostly, I pray what you begin to consume provides you with the energy you need to fight for freedom.

Priceless Knowledge

I can still remember the sickening feeling I had when I dropped a vase that my grandmother had given me. The vase shattered to bits, and my heart shattered with it. I couldn't react. I only stared at the vase while my mind tried to process what had happened.

The vase was a fun conversation piece. My granny loved to tell my guest how she had seen this particular vase on an antique appraisal program, and that the vase could sell for a pretty penny. I loved the vase because it reminded me of the day granny had given it to me. I could still see her smiling and carrying the beautiful lilies of the valley she picked from her garden. The vase may have been worth a considerable amount of money, but in my heart, it was truly priceless.

The vase, if it had survived, never changed its value based on whether I appreciated it or not. Its worth was never changed by the television show Granny had watched. Her knowledge of its worth is what changed.

It happens all the time though. Articles are often written about a person buying a junked art piece, only for the buyer to find out their art was worth millions. Again, the value of the item never changed. It was only the knowledge of its worth that changed.

Is it possible that like these treasures sold in everyday yard sales, you have been dismissed by others? If so, you're in good company. The same thing happened to David. His father, *his father*, dismissed him. As his brothers were lined up waiting for the anointing of oil over their heads, David's father never even bothered to invite David into the house. David was still tending to his sheep, possibly unaware anything out of the ordinary was happening. It took probing to discover David existed.

Albert Einstein was dismissed as an unintelligent child due to the fact that he was dyslexic. Many stories are like this, the greatest of the great are often overlooked before others become aware of their worth.

However uninformed and blind David's father may have been, David's purpose was predestined long before anyone ever knew. Similarly, God knew he would use Einstein in many ways, even if his teachers didn't see it. The worth of these fine men never changed, only the knowledge of who they were changed.

If you've seen the movie, *Hidden Figures*, you've seen the perfect illustration of dismissal turned into a vital component of history. The movie is based on the true story of three incredible ladies who did mathematical calculations for NASA. Katherine Johnson, Dorothy Vaughan, and Mary Jackson were quite brilliant and talented when it came to math. Nevertheless, they were not permitted to do more than their immediate task. Their knowledge was a fundamental element in space exploration. However, their story didn't begin that way. Their stories began with dismissal and discrimination.

These three ladies were part of an era in America's unfortunate history that said African Americans were less than, as were ladies. One more strike against them, and I'm doubtful NASA would have won the space race. The ladies were persistent and NASA relaxed their regulations over what information the ladies were permitted to access. This led to the astronomical feat of space exploration.

You're no different. If you've been dismissed, discounted, and underappreciated, take heart. Jesus was dismissed too. God knows your story and will finish writing it. Your job is to change the knowledge you possess about yourself. Could I suggest that like Dorothy

Vaughan, Mary Jackson, and Katherine Johnson you possess something great?

The dilemma is Satan is trying to inhibit your flight to higher ground. Dare I beseech you to recognize you've been granted access to higher spiritual knowledge. Know this: you're priceless. You're a real treasure. You may be counted out, dismissed, and denied now, but God is calling you priceless. And God is calling you to rise higher.

Masterpieces

"An attack on a nation's art is an attack on their true identity," my unsuspecting friend said (a friend I had only recently met. Okay, we hadn't made friends yet, but I felt such an incredible connection to this lady's mind. Surely, she must have been a someday, longtime friend). Regardless of titles and formalities, she had no idea what she had said to me. As we talked about wartime attacks on art, it occurred to me we have an enemy that without any hesitation will attack our nation's (a nation of kingdom heirs) true identity.

With natural conversation, we continued. We talked about books and the intentionality of colors. She told me about some books she had read and was reading. She mentioned *The Color Red* by Amy Butler Greenfield. She explained how the story of red evolved, a color. Interesting. A simplistic color. Red. A color that many take for granted, yet a color that has had many connotations of power and positions is absolutely intentional.

My friend told me of the attack on *The Golden Lady*, an art piece stolen during wartime. *The Golden Lady* was a painting that survived theft by Nazis and was later recovered by the rightful owners. I told my newly claimed friend of the artist, Matilda Lotz, only a child during the American civil war, who was shaped into her purpose by tragedy. Yet stolen works of art by Matilda during WWI proved to leave her in a deep and inescapable depression. Matilda sadly spent the remainder of her life seeking to find her works.

Though I tried, I could not settle my mind to one specific focus. One overwhelming thought, however, dominated my thought process. We are works of art created by God. For he carefully and intentionally planned our designs with great detail to our colors, shapes, and sizes. Of this, I am certain when he finishes each work, our father stands back to admire his creations smiles and says, "It is good!" (Genesis 1:31).

Yet if a person is unaware of their true identity, beauty, and design, they have little chance of ever being the royals God intended them to be. Just as the stolen artworks of history are mere streaks of paint in the wrong hands, your identity is void when left to the hands of our enemy. If one is not sure of the fact that they are a masterpiece (Ephesians 2:10), they cannot fully expect to escape the life of slavery our enemy has planned for us.

How could anyone be made in his image (Genesis 1:27) and be anything other than a nation's treasure? But when warfare strikes, the enemy invades the heart's home. He strips images away from the spirit rendering the soul hopeless, broken, and questioning its identity.

One must walk in the knowledge of themselves and in their identity as God's children purposed for more than slavery of Satan's design. To know the true value of something causes a person to protect that thing, even when the thing is our souls.

When warfare strikes, the soul, like young Matilda Lotz, has a chance to overcome and step into purpose. God has made you to be more than a mere slave to debt, strongholds, poor relationships, and other bastardized plans for your life. Satan has tried to force you to believe you must remain a slave. Has Satan tried to strip you of your identity? Have you been starving?

You're a masterpiece, a real work of art, an incredible work of art. Made with purpose, design, and above all intentionality. Each stroke of our Father's paintbrush was purposeful. As the color red has connotations of power and position, God purposed you for positions in his works.

As Matilda Lotz spent much of her time trying to regain her artwork possessions, you need to spend time regaining God's artwork. Like the rightful owner of *The Golden Lady* fiercely fought back to obtain their family's heirloom and identity, you must fight back to regain your purpose.

My youngest son once had a rubber bracelet given to him by his father. The bracelet was insignificant in appearance, but it meant something to my son. While on the bus one day, his bracelet was thrown out of the window by another kid.

My son was intent on getting his bracelet back. This meant we had to drive six miles to find it. I watched him get out of the car, and I honestly remember thinking, *How will you replace that when he can't find it? This will be a great night of tears.*

I was shocked when he walked around the tall grass, looked about for a few minutes, and then yelled, "Got it!"

If a small child can convince their mom to drive six miles, rummage through overgrown grass, late in the evening for a rubber bracelet given to him by his father, then why can't you do a little work to regain what your father has given to you? How much more valuable is your identity than a bracelet? Where is the harm in trying to regain and reclaim your identity and begin to learn how to walk as a royal?

Like Mother, Like Daughter

I once had a person look at my then two-year-old daughter and say, "She's beautiful. You don't think she looks like you, do you?" I'm going to hope that those words weren't meant to be ugly, but the sting of them took years to overcome. My daughter is now grown. I've obviously not forgotten these painful words. What's funny is that we're often told, "Wow, you guys look just alike." My daughter is gorgeous, but I always love to respond with, "Ha ha, you look just like me."

Have you considered the fact that when you don't see yourself as God does, it may be insulting to him? It is like saying, "He's beautiful. You don't look anything like your father, do you?"

Can you imagine how God feels when we deny him in our identity? He may be saying, "Hey wait, I made them in my image. I think they're incredible. That is my child, and your words are insulting." Saying anything negative about ourselves is similar to a census questionnaire that asks us to check anything denying our father's DNA.

The truth is, as with most, my personal history's pages could reveal many words spoken over me that I've had to learn how to repel. Life is a buffet, offering many varieties of painful things for us to chew on. But no different from standing in front of meal choices, we can decide not to digest what isn't good for us. Once you realize that not all things are truly good for you, you will have to decide they have no place in your spirit.

Nude Artwork

"Who told you that you were naked?" The words spoken to Eve by our father once seemed angry for my misguided heart. I think I misunderstood the text. I took it that God was angered by her knowledge. Now I'm convinced that he was angry but not as much with Eve as with the lie that something was wrong with her.

Nothing is wrong with the version of you that God created. But as Eve was lied to, you have been too. Learning your worth as artworks is valuable. Walking in truth and honesty of who you are created to be, that is priceless. No, I won't say that if you have some natural inclination to be mean, that's part of God's design. We have to bear fruit from living in a relationship with him. However, a bulldog drive that exists in you may be what speaks loudly to your purpose.

Have you been like Eve, lied to and now you're hiding who you really are? What you must understand is that God didn't design the sun to be dimmed. We designed sunglasses for our inability to handle its brightness. Don't dim who you are to cater to others. Use that inner being to foster what is to come.

Take Another Look

When I was small, our family spent Friday evenings in town, shopping. More specifically speaking, my mom spent Friday evenings shopping. The rest of us had other plans. My best friend and I terrorized the place. We played hide-and-seek and tag in the aisles. We made up fabulous store games (like find ladies undergarments and throw them over the aisles at the men standing around chatting). We went full speed until we were told it was time to leave.

Meanwhile, my dad would go to the pizza joint to order dinner and people watch. One evening, I waited with my dad as my friend didn't tag along, and my chances of finding solo mischief was slim to none.

This particular evening, my dad was watching someone walk by when he told me the words I pray to never forget. "If you take the time to look at anyone long enough, you'll find something beautiful about them."

Have you taken the time to look in the mirror for what beauties you possess? What about your emotional and spiritual mirror? Maybe you just need to take the time to look a little longer. Once you see the incredible beauty and purpose God has placed within you, then you will know you have finally looked long enough. And when you know the beauty you possess, when you know your identity, walking forward in victory will become much easier.

Focus Scriptures

For we are God's handiwork, created in Christ Jesus to do good works, which God prepared in advance for us to do. (Ephesians 2:10 NIV)

I praise you because I am fearfully and wonderfully made; your works are wonderful, I know that full well. (Psalm 139: 14 NIV)

Chapter 3

Feel the Burn
(Adversaries)

I'm too old, I thought to myself as I looked up to see a lady losing her mind and honking her horn at me. *I just don't care to travel on this road of strife with you, ma'am.* The soon-to-be aneurysm popping out of her forehead told me all I needed to know. The heckling woman wasn't feeling my observations of school zone speed limits. She passed, and whatever it was she was yelling at me was not, "Have a nice day." Regardless, I felt no urge to participate. Being the mildly passive-aggressive, not fully delivered Christian that I am, I smiled and waved.

I watched her storm off...only to land right next me at the red light. I giggled as I watched the tyrant turn right just to travel through three stop signs! All of her work was to avoid...waiting. Her efforts were thwarted. I arrived at the next light (green for me) just in time to watch her pull up perpendicular at the intersection for...a red light.

"Wear yourself out and hassle someone else, I ain't cha girl."

My morning had already proven to be a bit of a natural disaster. What the lady didn't know was that I had already ruined a child's day by asking him to get dressed for school. I had been awake for three hours before our encounter. It was a hit-the-ground-running kind of day. So the heart attack in waiting señorita was going to have to fight with someone else. I just wasn't having it.

As I drove home, I laughed a little about her attitude. She worked so hard to upset me. Still yet, she was the only person who she was wearing out. Meanwhile, she was getting nowhere with her negative behaviors.

What's interesting is, the woman who intended to let me have it only provided me with a lesson that I treasure. That is, no matter how negative another's actions are, they don't have to hinder your progress. This lady had no effect on my journey, just as some personal strife I had been facing, would not prevent me from moving forward in my life. Similarly, any strife you face on your journey, and you likely will face some discord, doesn't have to prohibit your progression.

Let's face it. Strife is an unfortunate part of life. And strife is much like starvation; it is a war tactic of your spiritual enemy. It is to distract you from purpose and intentionality.

However, strife can be a useful tool for growth. As you face opposition, you will learn it really isn't worth your energy to battle with others when you have a greater battle to win. And recognizing this is a victory in itself!

The Flip Side

To hear me tell the story above, you're only hearing one side. The lady who was so irritated by my driving may tell an entirely different tale. As most mothers know, the burned side of a grilled cheese is never to be seen by the children eating it, for obvious reasons, so that those picky littles will eat what they've been served.

On the journey to promise, during moments of discord, you don't necessarily have to be heard. You may get burned, and those who hurt you will possibly tell an entirely different tale. Those who hurt us often want their story to be more palatable. So they will sugar coat their side. They will hide the burns they inflict on you. You may find that they've told terrible things about you, and some things they say aren't remotely true. And it hurts. But you don't necessarily have to participate in a battle that isn't for you to fight. Keep your eyes set on the battles that further your purpose. You do not have time for distractions.

If you are in a season of discord and are the one getting burned or are in a fire, remember Shadrach Meshach and Abednego. They were placed in a fire by King Nebuchadnezzar. If you know the story, you know that sometimes our trial of fire is the only way God can be seen by others. King Nebuchadnezzar only saw God when the men were in the flames. You also know these brothers didn't have to do anything to defend themselves; God did it for them.

Furthermore, fire sometimes has a way of burning off the things that inhibit our purpose. (More on that in chapter 10.) The fire in the brother's case burned away their binding ropes. And you may be bound by some things God wants to remove. Just let him do his work.

I Can't

I once told a coworker to slow down as he was leaving work. I wanted him to pace himself to meet my needs of mockery. He had finished his work, and he was getting ready to leave. He hadn't done anything wrong. However, because other coworkers and I were going to have to work late, I wanted him to slow down for another nurse and myself to give him dirty looks.

"I can't," he responded with a smile as he kept walking. His response is the perfect reaction to give to strife, and I think it said it all. "I can't." I can't slow down because you're not going at the same pace as I am. I can't participate in retaliation or in your mockery. I can't be bothered by nonsense as I have somewhere I'm trying to go. Maybe you can even respond with "I won't."

My coworker's stance was like that of Paul. As Paul journeyed to Rome, he found himself to be shipwrecked. To make matters worse, a viper attacked him while he gathered wood for a fire.

Isn't that the way it goes? A person steps out to journey to the lands they want to stomp on, and somewhere along their path, they find themselves shipwrecked and, in the confusion of it all, bitten by the attack of a snake. Paul didn't stop though; he threw the snake into a fire and kept walking onward.

Satan is watching you. He wants to see you fail. And he will do all in his power to wreck your journey. In the middle of it all, he will attack, and he will use adversaries (vipers) to do his work. That's because he knows the power of the position you will stand on in your Promised Land.

You're learning how to fight him and how to become courageous; you're taking steps toward your future of freedom and likely purpose. The most important thing you can do is live like Paul and like my former coworker. Become so undistracted by Satan's plans that you're unwilling to allow a snakebite to derail your progress.

Satan will attack. When he does, as Paul did, throw him into the fire and proceed onward with your journey ahead.

Boo Hiss!

I suppose it is a stronghold of mine. The evidence only points to one conclusion; I enjoy watching others succeed. That isn't the stronghold. This is—in my weaknesses, I cannot watch others succeed without a little bit of harassment. It appears I have a tendency to heckle those I like, especially when I see them doing great things. Case in point, as follows:

Oh wow! Their yard is looking great, I thought to myself just before realizing the inevitable. I was going to have to give my new neighbors a real hard time for all their efforts. *I can't have this. I'm going to have to tell them to knock that off!* They were making my yard look real bad. And someone had to let them know. Otherwise, if they didn't dumb it down a little, I would have to step up to the plate on my yard. It only seemed like the fair thing to do. I walked out of my door to look at a nice yard. They, on the other hand, had to look at my neglected landscaping.

I know my yard didn't look bad because of anything my neighbors had done. Actually, most of what looked good in my yard was because of them. In their mercies, my neighbors had mowed for me on numerous occasions. Their landscaping looked good because of my neighbor's hard work and dedication. Mine, well, let's just say I'm the only reason it isn't up to par.

This is how it is with most progress. When a person does anything to better themselves or their lives, others start looking at their own lives and will often feel their grass isn't as green per se. Comparison is an ugly game to play. But a lot of people are champions at playing.

If you're making progress, it's possible there will be others who see you moving forward and will be forced to realize they're not. It isn't your fault they're not progressing any more than it is my neighbor's fault that I rarely work in my yard. And they certainly shouldn't have to water down their efforts because I hadn't done as much.

I may have wanted to heckle my neighbors in jest. But some will begin casting stones real fast when they see you advance toward your promises. If anyone is heckling you, it is likely related to the fact that your progress is forcing them to face their lack thereof. Don't water yourself down in order to satisfy those who aren't even in the same league.

The iron cowboy, James Lawrence, is quite possibly a psychopath. Okay, I'll reel it in. (I've warned you, I have weaknesses. I enjoy heckling.) He likely isn't a psychopath, but I will say Lawrence is a savage, a beast of an athlete who appears to challenge limits.

In 2015, Lawrence decided to do fifty ironman races in fifty states over fifty consecutive days. If you've watched the documentary, you know that while doing the 50/50/50 challenge, Lawrence had some health risks from over stressing his body. If Lawrence didn't slow down a little, he could have risked permanent or at least long-term damage to himself. Therefore, his team made the wise decision to have him do a few of the races in the gym setting.

The exercise was still being done. But those who were once his supporters began to criticize. How can anyone criticize a man who is doing fifty consecutive triathlons from their couches? It's more than any of them we're doing. It's simple; those who don't, love to criticize those who do.

Lawrence was hurt, and he did struggle with continuing. I'm sure that instead of feeling like he could complete his 50/50/50 challenge, he likely thought he had fifty reasons to stop. Still, the iron cowboy found new energy and was able to complete the challenge.

You may feel like the course in front of you is too hard. You may hear the boos from keyboard heroes and those you once believed would support you. And you may be hurting from it, but it doesn't mean anyone's opinion of you should stop you or even have the right to slow you down. Keep pressing forward.

The Pain of the Bite

So often freedom comes with the price of having those who will mock your progress and those who cannot understand you. Some will attempt to convince you that your choices are wrong. Like the road rage-driven lady mentioned before, some will disapprove of your speed.

The truth? Your purpose just may be bigger than what they can understand. But they don't have to understand it. They're not walking on your path.

When you find yourself facing adversaries, that doesn't mean you've wandered off the path toward victory. Adversity doesn't mean that you've left God's will at all. It may even mean that you're in the exact place that God wants you to be. He will use all that you face for your good and his glory (Romans 8:28).

Remember that the Israelites had to deal with Pharaoh, but when they arrived at the Promised Land, they had to claim victory over it. Once in the Promised Land, the Israelites had to battle for their promise. Any hardships faced while in wilderness seasons are designed to show you not just who God is but to train you how to claim your position in your promised land.

Your pharaoh (source of strife) may be chasing you down, but God is still on the throne. It may feel unfair that your pharaoh seems to continually gain ground. Imagine how the Israelites felt when they approached the Red Sea? Did they look at the sea and say, "Great! We've made it this far, and now our efforts will be thwarted by the sea"?

We know the rest of the story meant that God parted the sea and consumed Pharaoh's army. Have you considered whatever it is that is chasing you down, God will make an escape from? In the meantime, he may use the parted waters to wash away what doesn't belong on your journey. You have more in tow than you know. Is it possible that you want a Promised Land victory, but you're trying to tug along things that don't belong in the Promised Land? Do you carry pains of the past, friends who won't support your progress, bitterness, selfishness, comfort zones, etc. with you?

As scary as it may appear to see your faults and problems chasing you down, when the pains of the past, adversaries, strife are after you, God is positioning those things in places to be washed away.

Some painful experiences are the water needed to wash out what doesn't belong in your life. God uses experience and even pain to rid you of anything that isn't beneficial to your journey. In the next few chapters, we will explore what it is God may be asking you to leave behind as these things, and even people have no intended purpose in your Promised Land.

Focus Scriptures and Quotes

We are hard pressed on every side, but not crushed; perplexed, but not in despair; persecuted, but not abandoned; struck down, but not destroyed. (2 Corinthians 4:8–9 NIV)

Have I not commanded you? Be strong and courageous. Do not be afraid; do not be discouraged, for the LORD your God will be with you wherever you go. (Joshua 1:9 NIV)

Consider it pure joy, my brothers and sisters, whenever you face trials of many kinds, because you know that the testing of your faith produces perseverance. Let perseverance finish its work so that you may be mature and complete, not lacking anything. (James 1:2–4 NIV)

And we know that in all things God works for the good of those who love him, who have been called according to his purpose. (Romans 8:28 NIV)

A lion doesn't lose sleep over the opinion of sheep. (Various)

The loudest boos always come from the cheapest seats. (Babe Ruth)

Haters are like crickets. Crickets make a lot of noise, you hear it but you can't see them, then when you walk by them, they're quiet. (Israel Houghton)

True freedom is giving others permission to misunderstand you. (Lauren Daigle)

When you have a full understanding of who you are in God's eyes, you don't have to prove it to anyone else. (Steven Furtick)

Chapter 4

Forgetting What Lies Behind

In Exodus, Moses had an encounter with God. God instructed Moses to remove his sandals as Moses was standing on holy ground. God's promises for you are the holy ground he wants you to stand on. Just as airport security will often make people remove their sandals for security purposes, God may ask you to remove some things from your life for the security of maintaining your promises. As Moses was treading on holy land and had to remove what he previously stood on, God wants to remove the things you once stood on. (Those things may actually be idols that prevent you from seeing God is the one who will bring you to the promise.) Then and only then can you stand firm on the holy ground of his promises.

It will take time to see all that hinders your trip for what it is. But when you see your problematic obstacles, lay them down. Pay attention to God's warnings regarding what he is asking you to leave behind. Pray and ask God to help you to let go and transform you.

Consider the next several chapters as a packing guidebook. You must first empty your suitcase as you will need room to pack what is necessary for the Promised Land. This means you must remove "old wine" from your wine skins. This way once your luggage is empty you can appropriately pack what will be beneficial for your land of milk and honey. There is possibly more in your trunk than you're aware of. Let's unpack!

Pick a Lane

I'm far from super Christian. I lose my good graces more than I want to admit. But nothing makes me want to lose my Jesus more than people who insist on driving at snail speed in the fast lane. *Add angry tone.* Can you not see the five hundred and fifty cars behind you? Do you not understand that there are people in this world who do have places to go? They laud have mercy. *Beginning to yell.*

I mean really. Sigh. Some people have very little to no insight regarding the principles of traffic flow and moving out of another's way so that others can get where they're going. Come on. You don't necessarily have to hurry, just get back to the sloth lane so others can be on their way! And then there are those who aren't paying attention at all and are texting while driving.

Like the joys of driving with others who are so unaware of common traffic courtesy, there are times in life when we have to realize that someone may not be moving in the direction we're headed. They may not have the same intentions or purpose as we do. But that doesn't mean we should have to allow them to prevent our progress. And like it or not, there are others who will prevent you from getting where God designed you to go. At the very least, some folks will slow your progress to your destination if you allow them to share your fast lane. Other cats are deadweight, stumbling blocks. And if you allow them to stay in your lane, your journey to the Promised Land may become a lot harder.

Worst yet, some text while driving. These people are dangerous and oblivious to the risks they place those around them in. And some people are the same. They will derail you from ever making it to where you're supposed to go. They're like category five hurricanes leaving a wide path of destruction with ripple effects lasting for many years to come. Some are as detrimental to your journey as an iceberg to the titanic. But it wasn't necessarily the iceberg that sank the ship, instead it was the captain's unwillingness to heed iceberg warnings and take appropriate actions.

Though the decision to pass others and leave some behind is tough, sometimes we have to decide. Are there people in your life preventing you from progressing? If you know the ship is sinking, will you tie yourself to it? When you hear the iceberg warnings, will you change the path? Or will you sink the ship?

I once gave my youngest two options of things he wanted to do. He responded, "I don't want to pick a lane."

Honestly, most of us are no different. But if not choosing a lane prevents your walk, are you still interested in being double-minded? Will you choose to stay in a lane that prohibits you from moving into your destiny? Or will you go around obstacles that inhibit your advancement? Pick a lane.

Stumbling Blocks
The Islanders

No man is an island but some chose to live on them, isolated and unwilling to accept any form of help. Some want no part of change but a loving heart has a tendency to want to save all. That's not a bad thing. But if living on an island with the people you couldn't save prevented you from making it to your purpose or God's plans for your life, would you continue to stay? If staying on an island or trying to help a toxic person meant you could lose your life or if there was danger in helping, would you still insist on inhabiting this island? Or would you continue to keep the dangerous people in your life?

Any fine female (let's be honest most males too) who is going on a nice vacation wants to pack every item they own. As does any person on a journey to the Promised Land. It is a characteristic of a caring soul to want all that they love to go with them to their beautiful destination. However, just as ski suits do not belong on beach vacations, not everything or everyone belongs in your future.

God may ask you to forget what lies behind (that can be behaviors, attitudes, and even people) in order to press onward toward his promises. The problem for our hearts is that's hard to do, especially if the ones we leave behind are those we want to help the most. However, helping those who don't want to get better can become dangerous. Those who refuse to acknowledge dangers and refuse to progress are huge stumbling blocks. Those who stop your progression are detrimental, dangerous islanders.

I guess I should explain. An island off the coast of India is the perfect illustration for the necessity to leave what isn't profitable behind. This island is so dangerous that it is illegal to go there. The islanders are known to kill anyone who comes near. Even food drop offs and rescue efforts after a tsunami was considered to be a threat in islanders' eyes. Anyone who approaches this island is greeted with hostile attacks from natives, making this one of the most dangerous places on earth.

But it isn't just visitors who are at risk; natives are susceptible to their demise if outsiders come in. They've inhabited this island for years without outsiders. Visitors pose risks to native's safety due to the potential of bringing foreign microbes that could wipe out their entire tribe. Therefore, it is forbidden to go to the island.

Those who love wholeheartedly want to help all. They want to feed souls, house the homeless, dress the needy, slay dragons, and adopt all puppies and children as they should want to. But there are a few we cannot help. And when God asks us to leave them behind like the Indian government that says it is illegal to go to this island, God only has our best interest and safety at heart.

There are times when a person has to shed the weight of burdening people in order to press into the life God has for us. There are times when helping others becomes dangerous. How do you know? Pray and examine your heart. (Be willing to listen to answers God gives to your prayers.) Additionally speaking, examine reactions.

If you're trying to help someone and they meet you with daggers and arrows like the islanders mentioned above, it may be time to leave them in the past. This type of person is someone who blames you for their mistakes in order to protect themselves from accountability and progressing. This is a person who when you've addressed concerns for them or their behaviors and their well-being will shoot the arrows of accusations back to avoid accountability. A dangerous person cannot see their wrongdoings and possess a ride or die to them...mentality. They don't really even want friends. They want souls who enable their behaviors. Stay on their island, and eventually their arrows will injure you. This kind of person will also belittle you for doing the things you know God told you to do.

The path to your promised land isn't laced with eggshells you fear stepping on. You can walk island borders if you choose, but you will never make it away from the island by repeatedly journeying around the same obstacles. Islanders (metaphorically) are dead-weight, and choosing to take them to your next season could prove to be destructive to your destination.

Consider islanders as luggage. If you are to go into the wilderness for forty years, how much are you willing to carry? Are they still worth the burden of carrying their weight? Have you considered Moses likely would have wanted Pharaoh to go to the Promised Land with him? After all, he was raised in a home that he could easily have adopted affection for Pharaoh, but Pharaoh was dangerous. And Pharaoh was a stumbling block. Imagine what would have happened if Moses chose not to let go of the home he was raised in and took Pharaoh with him. It could have cost an entire nation's lives.

How do I identify an islander? Scenario one: your friend is participating in activities that don't settle well with your spirit. and they want to involve you in their actions. You are, one, uncomfortable with the actions, and, two, you feel like you should have not been asked to participate in the first place. A safe person should be approachable.

You tell your friend that the requests make you uncomfortable. A safe person should have the insight to recognize this shouldn't happen in the first place. However, if they did do so, they would examine their actions and correct the inappropriate behavior or at least leave you out of their actions.

Contrary to safe people, an unsafe "friend" shoots the arrows of projection at you. "Your self-righteousness is unbelievable. I know what mistakes you've made." This alone is enough to show you the islander is dangerous. But they will give you more evidence of their dangerous habits as you find yourself feeling the inevitable need to vacate their island. Unfortunately fleeing this island will carry the burden of more daggers being thrown as you paddle your boat to safety.

You will find this person loves to rub your nose in any mistakes you've ever made; this helps them to avoid admitting their actions were inappropriate. Be prepared for it to get worse as island inhabitants will remind you of all they've ever done for you, suggesting that you're unappreciative because you refuse to participate or enable their hurtful actions. This is the manipulation spirit of a slave owner. They feel as though they're entitled to your attachment because of the codependency they believe they see in you.

Just imagine shedding them as a weight-loss mission. Losing weight is typically not as fun as packing it on. Sometimes the taste of something is far more delightful if it carries the promise of staying on our hips for a while. Try to shed just one pound and sound the trumpets—it's craving time.

Shedding others who prove to be unhealthy for us, well, that is an entirely different game, and it's a hard one to play. But as weight loss is better for our overall health, losing those who aren't good for us will prove to be beneficial in the long run.

Be prepared. These dangerous islanders. They're some of the hardest people to shed. The daggers they throw, they're hard to dodge. These people have spent an entire lifetime learning unfair ways to fight. They've learned the only way to communicate is to shoot the painful arrows (typically of your weaknesses) at others.

Imagine that you approached an island where you wanted to help those who seemed to be in need. Natives studied you and allowed you in. *Great*, you think to yourself as you begin ministering to their spirits, *I'm in!* However, as you spend time on the island, you begin noticing the behavior of the natives is questionable. Worse yet, you start taking on attitudes of the natives and acting in ways that go against your innate beliefs. Your heart feels sick, and you notice you have taken on a bit of depression. *This isn't as good for me as I thought. I must leave this island.*

Now natives recognize you as one of them, and they don't want you to leave. Remember this island is savage, and the residents have spent their entire existence learning how to fight, hunt, and attack. Just as they feel threatened by outsiders, they feel threatened by your departure. And they will not have it.

When leaving dangerous folks behind, the unfortunate truth is, they won't make it easy. At all. They will begin sharpening their daggers and shoot them the minute they see you begin to leave. They've had time studying you now that you made it into their circle, so they now know your downfalls. And these group of dangerous people are willing to shoot all their weapons if it creates a fear of leaving within you.

Be prepared to hear mocking of your relationships with others, especially with God. Expect to feel the painful piercings of their arrows of accusations. Be prepared to feel the sting of their manipulative daggers hitting as you float away to safety. Just remember you're headed toward safety. The sting of their daggers is far better than staying. It will take time to see the peaceful fruit from leaving, but it is worth it.

As mentioned above, on the real island, outsiders can be dangerous to Sentinelese people. Similarly, if you stay around some people, you can become dangerous to them. If you start trying to prove your worth to them or mission, if you fall into the trap of wanting to show them the way, you can lose the ability to help them at all. Your words may pierce them. Sometimes it is better to walk away. Sometimes it is better to recognize some battles aren't yours to fight.

Perennials vs. Annuals

Similar to the above mentioned but not as unfortunate, we can often see the beauty of a person or a season and want to pack that part of our lives to take with us to the next season.

But not everything or everyone gets to go. The weight is just too heavy. Airplanes can't carry more weight than they're designed to carry. Carrying more than their weight limit can cause airplanes to crash. You're coming to a season where you're expected to fly higher, so you have to lose some weight. Even if some of the things you carry are beautiful.

Imagine a beautiful fence laced with pansies. Each flower happily welcomes any passerby. The flowers are beautiful, but they're only made to be enjoyed for one season of life. They're annuals.

Disappointed in the time frame we've been given to enjoy this beauty God has given us, we want to take the flower into the next year. The problem is that isn't God's design.

Sometimes we have to understand some people or jobs or periods of our lives are the same as annual flowers. They're beautiful. They are a gift. We don't have to deny their beauty to let them go. But they aren't made for more than a small season. There are friends and loved ones who are like shooting stars. When you see them, you know it was a gift. You may admire its beauty, but shooting stars are only to be admired momentarily. You can thank God for the gift, but you can't contain it or keep it.

Letting go isn't easy, but in time, God will help you to press onward toward what he has in store for you. Just because someone doesn't go to the next season with you doesn't mean it has to end on a bad note. It only means they were not made to go where you are going.

It's often said that a fish can only grow to be as big as the fish's environment. Contrary to this belief, genetically speaking, fish will grow to their predestined size despite their environment. However, like plants with improperly sized containers, some environments are dangerous to fish. When a fish isn't in the correct environment, the fish can end up stunted and even die.

We are no different. We have to surround ourselves with people that are of a safe-growing environment. Sometimes leaving others in the past is necessary to create the proper environment for growth and development. Sometimes the only way we are able to keep people is to keep them in our prayers but leave them in God's hands and leave them in our past.

The question is, "Are you willing to lay them down and trust God with them? Are you willing to forget what lies behind to press onward to God's plan for your life?"

Buzz Onward

I have a strange affection toward bees. In faith, they represent how a Christian should live. (Working diligently for the hive/kingdom.) Oddly, I find them to be beautiful creatures. Despite my affections for bees, I don't have any desire to cater to these little hitchhikers while I'm driving.

However, one bee did not share my feelings and decided my car was an optimal way to travel. It does seem reasonable factoring in the travel ability of their tiny wings; my car may actually be favorable means of transportation.

I was traveling down I-40 near work when I noticed this little guy on my window. I work an hour from home. And I wanted to let the bee out of my car when I got to work. I had a moment of pause though. I was concerned about the bee's ability to survive without his original hive.

Unfortunately, I couldn't leave him in the car. It would *bee* (yes, ridiculous pun intended) too hot for my little friend in my car. He wouldn't survive. I had to release him in a new environment.

Is it possible that you're no different? You've made it too far from your original position. You may miss those you've left behind and wish to return to the hive. But God also knows that if he leaves you where you are, your survival isn't likely. Sometimes the hard painful truth is God loves you too much to leave you where you are. He knows how far you've come. So he will place you in a season or place that is optimal for your survival.

Focus Scriptures

Warn a divisive person once, and then warn them a second time. After that, have nothing to do with them. You may be sure that such people are warped and sinful; they are self-condemned. (Titus 3:10 NIV)

Jesus turned and said to Peter, "Get behind me, Satan! You are a stumbling block to me: you do not have in mind the concerns of God, but merely human concerns." (Matthew 16:23 NIV)

And it will be said: "Build up, build up, pre-
pare the road! Remove the obstacles out of the
way of my people." (Isaiah 57:14 NIV)

Do not be misled: "Bad company corrupts
good character." (1 Corinthians 15:33 NIV)

Chapter 5

Shedding Weight

Who doesn't love a good renovation? So many of us will eagerly watch renovation programs on the tele. It's enjoyable to see something that could be discarded turned into a treasure.

Is it possible that God looks at your life like it is a renovation project? You may see a dump; he may see something worth flipping. You may see rusty nails; he sees hidden treasures and unrevealed beauty.

On these renovating shows, there is occasionally a person or two who aren't really comfortable with letting go of the mess. They may see grandma walking across their dilapidated floor and feel as though she is still there. The challenge in these situations is for the designer to gain the homeowner's trust.

If your life is a flip in progress than you must know like a historical home being turned to treasure, you're going to see some old things discarded. Rotten floor, let it go. Broken heart, let him repair it.

There is no reason to hoard negative emotions any more than there is a purpose to hoard trash in your living room. In seasons of transformation, it will feel like God is ripping apart your entire world. And he is. But he has a plan for the mess. He has a design in mind for every room in your heart, mind, body, and soul, for your entire life and existence.

The challenge for God is gaining your trust. Do you trust the designer of your life enough to allow him to remove what doesn't belong on your journey? Can you let go of what doesn't belong so that he can really create something new for you?

Letting Go of Stinky Gross Dumb Stuff

Did you know that frog's eyes bounce? It's true. How do I know this bizarre bit of information? Easy. I went to school with the gross species of the male Homo sapiens.

In seventh grade, I believe, like many schools, it was a requirement to dissect a frog. I hated this assignment. It wasn't necessarily gross, but the smell got to me. I dreaded doing this assignment almost as much as I hated dissecting a squid. That was beyond odoriferous.

But the boys, those disgusting beings, they looked forward to doing this task. Weirdos. It was like their eyes, ew eyes, lit up the minute they found out they would get to cut a frog. Why? Because frog's eyes bounce.

It was a rite of passage. Each boy would happily pull their frog's eyes out of their pockets to bounce them on the floor. I remember the joy on one boy's face as he had my "yes" to taking my frog's eyes.

I have later wondered if those boys actually learned anything other than the bouncing properties of the amphibian's eyes. I'm not sure I learned anything if I'm being completely transparent.

My question is, "What if they choose to keep the entire frog for some other reason? Why in the world would they do that?" Well, why would anyone choose to keep something so nasty around? Imagine the smell of decaying amphibious bodies kept for amusing purposes alone.

In life, we have assignments we just don't want to do. Others may light up with joy based on their enthusiasm for these assignments. But truth be told, God will give us assignments we don't particularly find to be anything less than stinky, but he has a purpose for them.

For instance, God may not have caused some bad things in your life, rather Satan did. But when God allowed it, he likely meant to use it as a teaching opportunity.

Let's say someone wronged you. That can be an opportunity to pray for discernment. It can be a chance to learn the difference between being a doormat and being assertive. This could be something that is God showing you about yourself. So many lessons can come from stinky situations. That's the serving purpose of these trials.

But sometimes we choose to hold onto our anger, hurt, bitterness, and so on instead of the lessons. When this happens, there becomes an imbalance. Imagine keeping the dissected frog. Eventually that would become a real nasty mess. And it would *smell!* Bitterness, anger, unforgiveness, and resentment are decaying emotions. And what they decompose is the person who carries these feelings. God didn't ask us to bear this kind of weight.

It's okay to dissect why you allowed someone to mistreat you. It's okay to get to the root of problems. It's okay to use any situation as a learning moment. But holding onto begrudged feelings is holding onto something that is dead. It is okay to learn from situations without keeping the mess. Hoarding wrongdoings and bitterness isn't the purpose of the assignment. I'm not saying we have to pretend that something didn't happen. But keeping the mess not the education involved won't help you in any form.

The road to the Promised Land will require forgiveness. And laying down what isn't good for your designed purpose is a must. I can't urge you enough to pray and ask God to help you to lay down the smelly emotions of unforgiveness, bitterness, and anger. It's hard, but it's worth it.

Wrecked

I was once driving on I-40 and needed to get off the interstate. I looked over my shoulder and saw a car was in my blind spot. It was good that I looked back instead of relying on my mirror. The man who was in my blind spot was determined not to let me over. When

I would slow down, he did the same. When I sped up to get in front of him, he matched my speed. He made it impossible to merge.

I looked back again to speed up so that I could get around him. Looking in his direction was wise. Unfortunately, I kept my eyes on him too long. As I turned around looking forward, the lady in front of me had slammed her breaks. I tried to stop, but it was too late. I crashed into her.

I wasn't wrong to watch for other cars in another lane. I wasn't wrong to look before merging. The mistake I had made was that I looked back too long.

Life will offer us obstacles like the unrelenting man who refused to allow my move. He wasn't my favorite person ever. In all transparency, I didn't offer him friendly nicknames of my affections. But no matter how the lane hog of my yesterday acted, my actions of having my eyes on what was behind me, and what was happening in another lane caused me to wreck.

In life, some will just be nasty. Period. Keeping your eyes on another lane or on what is behind you can cause you to crash as you're trying to move forward. The cost is too much. Sometimes our only option is to let go of what lies behind, to press onward toward what is ahead.

Fear

I can't remember any greater fear than what I felt the few times I had finally pushed my normally easygoing parents too far. One of these moments came when I wouldn't stop arguing with my brothers as our family ascended up the side of a mountain headed home. My mom finally had enough.

She pulled over on the side of the twisty deserted road, "*Get out!*"

"What?" I innocently replied.

Surely, she wasn't talking to me, her precious and delicate child. I would never survive the walk home. Sun beat down on my dry chapped lips. I was destined to get lost. Add dramatic sting. I would starve. The elements would be too harsh (wind howling), and I would certainly shrivel up into nothing but mere buzzard food.

"*Get out*," she repeated. "Stop it. Shut up or get out."

Wow. Harsh ramifications for innocently sitting in the backseat doing nothing but minding my own business. Ouch.

I rarely pass this particular area without being reminded of that very moment. The moment when the fear of God was instilled in me by the most passive Mother Theresa of a lady ever. The drive home was silent. I didn't say another word.

"Was she serious? Would she have left me to my bitter cold grave?" I still ask myself these stark unsettling questions to this day. Sweat dripped from my forehead. I certainly wasn't taking any chances. I shut my face up. I was glad too. I wouldn't be here today if I didn't.

Fear is the same as my mouthy, oh wait, innocent little self. Fear won't hush until you make it. It's likely that as you travel onward toward your promises, you will hear the nagging voice of fear whispering in your ear. It's doubtful that there will ever be a moment on the journey that fear doesn't try to hitch a ride. But like my saintly mother, you must let it know you're not willing to listen to its incessant chatter anymore. When it comes to fear, you must say, "*Shut up or get out.*"

My grandfather used to laugh at my fear of spiders. "Why? You're bigger than it is. It's more scared of you than you are of it." Fear is similar to an ugly little spider. I promise fear is more scared of you than you are of it. Squash it.

Doubt

I once watched as a longtime friend joined me on a new job. We had worked together on a busy floor in a hospital for eight years before this. I had been in a new position for about a year and was so excited to have her on our team.

I had seen her in action. She was one of the best nurses I had ever known. When I was a novice, she was my beacon in the storms of fear that new nursing brings. I would have never helped her get the new position had I not known her to be a rock star nurse. So I had a moment of confusion when she reported discomfort and almost seemed afraid in this new role.

I had seen a hero on her stomping grounds but forgot to give her the courtesy of a discomfort allowance. She was in new territory so naturally she wasn't comfortable. I sure wasn't comfortable when I had arrived, so why was I so confused by her discomfort? She was still very afraid. It was like watching a beaten dog deciphering if a new owner was safe. She had been conditioned to believe in fear as our former position was one of constant fear.

Once I remembered the PTSD feelings I had experienced while transitioning to the new place, I was able to back up. I could give her courtesy to slowly wade into the position. I realized her heart was still afraid. As I would want to say to a battered pup, I wanted to tell her, "You're safe here." I tried to show her, but I knew she would have to see it for herself. Eventually she would grow comfortable and see this was a place she could enjoy.

The truth is my friend's posture may have said one thing, "fear." But her actions had already said another, "courage." She didn't wait until she felt safe to leave; she did so knowing the ground she was already on was not where she belonged anymore. She didn't know what was ahead, but she sure knew she didn't want to be part of the enslaved place she was living in before.

I wanted to remind her of all the things I knew about her and how I always saw her as a role model. I encouraged her as much as I could. But more importantly, I prayed for her. I knew the feeling of discomfort she had. My greatest concern though was that due to discomfort she didn't find comfort with her former captors. That the discomfort of the new land didn't make the chains of her past seem comfortable enough to place them back on her wrist.

God has seen something in you. That is why he chooses to bring you out of slavery and is taking you to the Promised Land of your freedom. Like my view of my friend, God looked at you in the lineup and said, "I pick them. I know they possess determination and ability. They're rock stars. I've seen them in action, and I want them on my team."

But like my friend's transitional period, this new life you're stepping into will take some time to adjust to. You will need to remember it took forty years for the Israelites to make it. It will take some time for you to adjust to the mentality that you're not made to be a slave. Time is the required price of stepping into identity and purpose. Time is what it takes to travel to freedom.

While it's possible that you may be feeling like my friend, you may be covered in fear. Every step you've taken thus far says different. It isn't that you're doing anything wrong, not at all. But instead, it's that coming from an enslaved period into the wilderness is just confusing. Perhaps you believed leaving one place you would find comfort and ease in the other. But this is transition. And transition brings the joys of doubt and uncertainty. Your sword against doubt is faith, and you will need to use that sword fight against stagnancy.

Square Peg in a Round Hole

All of us do it, even if we're conscious of the fact or not, we try to fit square pegs in round holes. The problem? They just don't fit. If you don't believe me, start watching for this phenomenon the next time you're in a social setting.

People will ask, "What do you do for a living? What degree do you have? What school did you go to?" The list is continual for miles on miles. What I see happen in these situations all too often is, though some truly just want to know about you as a person, others are summing up the level of respect they want to give a person by what it is they "do" or who they presume that person to be.

Whether we like it or not, the dilemma that exists here is that prestigious schools no more make a man than the lack thereof. Fame is no indicator of clout or respect. Historical mishaps do not determine future prospects for better living.

Society places round holes around lives and spirits. Unfortunately, some never stop trying to fit their (square) spirits into societal holes.

But when freedom steps in, life begins. By that, I mean, when a person gives themselves permission to be what it is they feel drawn to be, slavery no longer has its stronghold.

Have you ever watched a person redefine themselves? It's beautiful. It appears as though a real mess is occurring to the misguided eye. Quite the opposite is true. For example, a person who has lived a corporate life may suddenly abandon the lifestyle, begin wearing tie dyed clothing, and dump their entire life savings into starting a mom and pop restaurant.

For an unaware soul, it would appear the person has finally gone off the deep end. Untrue, they likely found out the truth, life is short, and the best way to miss it is by being the wrong form of oneself. A heart who tries to fit into another person's preconceived concept of themselves is a life wasted.

There is freedom in letting go of the concept that you have to fit into someone else's idea of who you are. You're not a round peg. Or maybe you are. But the shape of you is to be determined by you. You have to start feeling the freedom to be you.

Comparison

When I was in grade school, a boy in my class kept cheating off of my papers. Though I liked the guy as a person, his cheating was very frustrating to me. I was putting in the work; he was getting my grade.

One day, I decided I had enough and came up with a plan. I wrote all the incorrect answers down and waited for him to turn in his work. When he turned his paper in, I changed my answers and then turned in my work. He failed that assignment. I didn't.

I actually feel some misplaced guilt to this day for what I did. I somehow want to track the guy down and ask him if he had ever forgiven me. I'm sure he hasn't lost any sleep over it, but the little girl in me feels bad.

In life, we tend to find ourselves looking at other people's lives and wondering why we're not happy in our lives. It's because we're looking at someone else's answers. And the truth is, they may have one answer that you see and something they change when you're not looking.

You're only seeing the surface. I've seen it more than I would have ever wanted to. Imagine a woman posting on social media that her husband is the most amazing man ever. She got all kinds of likes. You wished you had a marriage like theirs. You even prayed for it. But what those who read her posts, including you, didn't know is that her words were empty. Her home behavior is atrocious. She calls her husband anything but a good man to his face. She chastises every move he makes. She runs around on him with several men. It may seem confusing, but the truth is simple, she changes her answers when you're not looking.

Imagine another woman whose social media profile was all you ever wanted. You follow her to learn how to become a top selling business guru like her. She juggles life and family like a champ. If only your children had perfectly pressed clothing and hair like her children. But you can't seem to even get the laundry to the dryer without it souring better yet keep your kids smiling for every single picture.

How is it that she runs a business and has such a clean house anyway? The thing is, she isn't posting the part of the pictures where she is yelling at the kids to smile. She didn't post pictures of her mess. (I'm actually a little bothered by those pictures that never have messes. Does anyone have fun in that house, better yet even live there?) Your social media friend isn't posting stories that tell you how she almost went bankrupt on the journey to success. She isn't telling you what her success cost. She isn't telling you that it almost or maybe even did cost her a marriage. She isn't telling you that she's tired of the facade. She isn't telling you that she hasn't had a good night's sleep for a while because she has to work so much. She's changing her answers. Or maybe she is hiding a little of her truth.

You want their success. Even if their success was easily earned, their race isn't yours to run. The problem with a comparison approach is, you're not doing your assignment when you're busy looking at other people's work. Keep your eyes on your own work. It isn't that we shouldn't try to succeed and surround ourselves with those who do well. We should "iron sharpens iron." But we have to run our own race that God has set before us. That is the key to passing your assignment.

Comfort Zones

I imagine it was hard for the Israelites to leave what they left behind. They had no idea what was ahead of them. They may not have liked what Pharaoh did to them, but Pharaoh was a comfortable enemy. They knew their city. They knew where to find the things they wanted. The Israelites knew who their neighbors were. But leaving meant the men and women of Moses's day would face the unknown. Leaving meant exchanging comfort for uncertainty.

But comfort is an enemy to progression. Comfort zones will inhibit growth and keep you deep in the smelly waters of stagnancy. Part of progressing toward your promised land is learning how to get out of your comfort zones. God will give you promptings to speak to those you would never speak to. He will ask you to do things that you would never dream of doing prior to the uproar of change. He will expect you to place fear aside and walk in faith.

But he has a purpose to these promptings. When God asks you to step out of your comfort zones, he is preparing you to be Promised Land ready. For instance, if God is asking you to speak at a small event, he may be preparing you to operate in the Promised Land in ways you don't realize are coming. If you feel a push to apply and interview for a job you would never have chosen, God may have purpose. Even if you didn't get that particular position, the interview could be a preparation for another position later. If God is asking you to volunteer at a shelter, he may have the promised spouse there waiting to meet you. But part of the promise of a spouse in your life is that God expects the two of you to further his kingdom by doing outreach together.

You may not be comfortable operating in a way that God prompts you to do. If this is you, maybe a reminder of Jonah's disobedience will help you to step out in faith. If you choose fear over faith, I hope you will choose fear of what you will miss if you don't operate in faith.

Anxiety

Standing in the room with a lady I briefly encountered proved to be somewhat anxiety producing. Her television blared as the politically charged discussion panel of hosts argued their points. Like most of these style programs, all participants yelled over one another unconcerned with the other's opinions or beliefs. All that was of importance to any of them was their stance on the matters. As the host screamed at one another, I heard the lady in the room with me say, "I hate shows like this. It is all so negative. They don't focus on anything but what is bad. I'm telling you, it makes my blood pressure rise."

While I agreed with her dislike toward these particular types of programs, I felt a tad bewildered. The remote was immediately to her right side. Why didn't she simply pick up the control and change the channel? I wasn't entirely convinced of her disdain. Did she really dislike the programming? Or was it possible that she didn't find the taste of the programming to be pleasant, but she found the noise to be of greater comfort than the silence she would experience if she chose to turn the tele off all together? Regardless, her actions and her words spoke in opposition to one another.

Anxiety is very similar to the loud host of political shows. Anxiety wants to choke out any word spoken by the opposing belief. Still yet, complaining tele hosts rarely accomplish anything (other than causing strife and securing jobs for the blood pressure medication industry). Anxiety is loud and rambles on, never producing anything but negative results. In no way will I say it isn't real; anxiety is a very real and sometimes disabling feeling. I won't discredit those who experience anxiety, nor will I say that medications for such and therapists aren't of any benefit. However, when it comes to moving forward into your purpose, you have to say, "I have the controller. It is time to change the channel."

Selfishness

If you've lived long enough in a region where Bradford Pears are popular, you've seen how they will spontaneously break. The reason for this is due to the fact that the tree has several branches growing from the same area. The branches grow too large and compete for nutrients and room to grow. Where one branch doesn't give way, the others eventually will break off unable to get what they need to survive. Apparently, the tree has more detrimental issues tied to it. Bradford pears will prevent other surrounding trees from surviving as well. The Bradford pear is an invasive species.

Selfishness is like a branch on the Bradford pear; it will choke out survival of any other limb. When you focus so much on your selfish desires, you starve others from having what they need. This way of existence can cause others to starve, to fall away from lack of valuable life God wants to give them. A selfish life like the Bradford pear looks beautiful on the surface but offers very little to anything around it. Invasive selfishness left untamed will take over causing a path of destruction leaving others to wither.

God isn't looking to bring you to the Promised Land only to save your tail. He wants you free, but he also is planning to use you for his glory. Therefore, he must work on you in the wilderness to remove the selfishness that resides in all of our hearts. God will remove selfishness from his children so that his work can be done through them. If we are less selfish and we offer space for other branches to gain nutrients (help others with the knowledge of God), then a beautiful scene can be painted.

Worry

I adore my younger brother. Regardless, facts are facts, and brothers know how to anger us. Even when they don't mean to. Years ago, this was the case when my brother was over. "I have never seen anyone work so hard to get nothing done." He was hanging out at the house while I was cleaning. (Let me add a little note to the men reading, just don't. These are words you shouldn't say to a lady who is falling to bits trying hard to achieve just one task before the day is done.) I was stressed trying to accomplish more than I was able. Truth be told, he was probably right. I likely wasn't accomplishing a thing. My efforts weren't of much benefited purpose. But did he really just say that? Jerk.

Are you working hard to accomplish nothing? This is worry's purpose. It's to cause you to stay busy without ever accomplishing a single thing. You can worry all day long about how your future will look. Meanwhile, you will spend your today on what may or may not happen. There is no benefit to worry. You may read the words I'm saying to you and respond similarly to my initial reaction to my brother, "Really? Jerk."

But it's true. It doesn't matter how much you worry about your bank account; worry doesn't add money to it. It won't benefit your future to worry about if you're doing the right job today. Your children will never become better human beings by your misplaced parental guilts. If you're trying and praying, you're doing what's right. To worry about anything is to make that thing greater than God.

Worry is another thing you're going to ask God to help you unpack.

Any of the types of people, feelings, or behaviors and stumbling blocks listed in the last few chapters, they're something all people can expect to encounter at some point in their lives. However, we do have to lay down what lies behind in order to obtain the beauty God has in store for us.

I once had a rosemary plant that began looking unhealthy and wilting. I didn't really know what was wrong with the plant, but I knew that leaving it next to my mint plant could risk losing the mint plant as well. When I moved the rosemary plant away from the other household plants, I began working to save rosemary. Finally, I had to call it quits with rosemary as I was unable to save it. I wasn't sure why, but I felt God prompting me to let go of this plant.

Meanwhile, a precious lady who I worked with was being prompted by God to do a greater purge. She knew I loved plants, and she had an incredible green thumb. She came to work and told me she "had a few plants that she needed to thin out." She offered them to me. Little did I know the "few plants" she had would fill my entire mom van. It took some time before I could even figure out where to fit them all in my home. I was elated with my new problem. Then one day, as I stood watering those beautiful plants and thanking God for all the lessons he gave me through them, I felt him speak. God showed me that what he wanted to give me required letting go. I later dissected my rosemary and found bugs eating the roots. If I had not gotten rid of the infected plant, it is possible the new beautiful plants would have become infected as well.

There is nothing God will prompt you to let go of that isn't of greater benefit. It is possible that like the bugs eating my rosemary plant, anything he is trying to take away, will ruin what he is trying to give you.

Additionally, refusing to let go of what isn't beneficial to your journey will prevent new and good fruit from growing. When I was younger, my grandfather was like the friend I previously mentioned. He had an amazing green hand, not just a thumb. I was young and attempting to grow my first garden. I went away for a week and came home to find my squash had stopped producing. I told my papaw about the problem, and he told me that "some plants are like a nursing mother. Once you stop getting what you need from them, they believe their job is done and stop producing."

Similarities exist here; your life is no different from plants. If you want to produce anything, you need to create flow. Pick off old things to create new ones.

Small Thinking Produces Small Living

Have you ever seen a lady who is built with a larger frame wearing tiny shoes? You can clearly see the shoes she is wearing are too small. She looks uncomfortable. You can see each step causes pain. As you watch her, you fear she's going to fall due to the inappropriate size of those gorgeous high heels. It's obvious she is busting out of the top of the shoe. If you can see it, why can't she?

Some things are just too small for our future. Some things won't fit. They may be cute and attractive. But wearing them can cause a person to fall. Walking with something too small is painful, not beneficial. It's like putting lawn mower tires on a dump truck. It just isn't going to work. You're just not built for small thinking or small-minded people. Sorry.

As you thin out your company and emotional closet, consider the perspective of a child. I once held up an old coat up and asked my youngest child if it still fit. I looked at the coat and read the tag, "Size four. We'll give it to a kid who doesn't have a coat." His protested "no" shocked me. He had plenty. Furthermore, he was now seven years old, and there was no way that coat would fit him. We are no different than my youngest in that we have moments that we refuse to let go of what doesn't fit anymore.

Honey, you've outgrown these things of the past. You're coming into a new season. It's time to let go of the things that are no longer useful. Child, lay them down. As you journey through your wilderness, leave these things of the past with Pharaoh.

Focus Scriptures

Brothers and sisters I do not consider myself yet to have taken hold of it, but one thing I do: Forgetting what is behind and straining toward what is ahead. I press on toward the goal to win the prize for which God has called me heavenward in Christ Jesus. (Philippians 3:13–14 NIV)

Have I not commanded you? Be strong and courageous. Do not be afraid or discouraged for the Lord your God is with you wherever you go. (Joshua 1:9 NIV)

The Lord himself goes before you and will be with you. He will never leave you nor forsake you. Do not be afraid: do not be discouraged. (Deuteronomy 31:8 NIV)

Chapter 6

Counterfeit

There appears to be a recipe to high end restaurant landscaping. Stonewalls, cherry bar tops, perfected lighting, strategically placed mirrors, a water feature here, fire accents there, the later, two are even better when in combination living within the same living space.

No matter how beautiful the space may be if your fifty-dollar plate tastes like it was cooked by a ten-year-old, you have a counterfeit version of what you hoped to receive. It is no different from the disappointment one would experience when going to some concerts.

It doesn't matter how many pyrotechnics effects are used, if music quality is lacking, the show may not be worth attending. Extravagant lights don't increase the musical talents of a band.

When one pays for anything, their expectations are that they will receive what they were willing to shell out money for, especially when the price tag is a higher one. Unfortunately, when it comes to promises, counterfeits exist.

Counterfeit versions of the people and promises who should be in your Promised Land will present themselves to you. Satan wants to hijack your trip to purpose. If he can't derail your spirit, he will send counterfeit versions of those who actually belong on your path to distract you and to keep you from making it to the promises of God. These counterfeit versions are people or even "opportunities" that will look very similar to what God has been teaching you do belong on the path. But they are more destructive than the people and opportunities you know you shouldn't be around. They're incognito, and it's occasionally hard to recognize a counterfeit. As accepting counterfeit bills would be unprofitable to your bank account, accepting counterfeit people, jobs, etc. will prove to bankrupt your spirit. But how can you tell if someone or something is legitimately safe?

As paper currency has some telltale signs that it shouldn't be accepted, people do too. Opportunities for change, like people, can seem very enticing as well. However, these can easily be counterfeit versions of your Promised Land. Let's look at counterfeits versus safe allies and see if we can learn how to distinguish the difference.

First, let's take a moment to define counterfeit. It is anything made in exact *imitation* of something *valuable* or *important* with the *intention to deceive.*

Make no mistake about it. Satan will offer you imitations of what is actually valuable and important to your journey. Above all note this, his intent is to deceive you or defraud God's plans for your life. The enemy wants to derail your train to glory. As you've been learning the importance of unpacking dead weight, Satan has been studying what it is you do want or have been promised in order to stop your progress. He's been crafting counterfeit versions of God's promises to prevent you from having what is truly valuable.

"Ouch! You mean to tell me I've come this far only to question if what I'm getting is true?" *Yes!* But I'm telling you this with one hope, that is you find what is real and of God. That hope is that you will accept nothing shy of God's best plan for your life. My sisters and brothers, my heart's desire is that you will only accept what is truly valuable to your next beautiful season.

Okay, we have established that there are those we can recognize as dead weight. But how can we tell if something or someone is counterfeit? According to businessknowhow.com, large counterfeit bills are often passed by those who are wearing nice suits. These particular criminals dressed the part of businessmen; therefore, they're never questioned. Counterfeit promises will dress the part in hopes you will never question their worth.

Businessknowhow.com is a good source for imitation money recognition. We're going to use the same counterfeit, spotting principles combined with what truths we know from God. We will do so to understand what does belong on the path to the Promised Land and how to spot the fakes.

Scrutiny

Be forewarned, deciphering authenticity is sometimes tough. The truth is, we want everyone to have our hearts and be trustworthy. Before reading one more word, I ask you to understand this fact: Those who are trying to pass counterfeit versions of anything do not appreciate being questioned. In no circumstances am I promoting the idea that all are proven guilty until otherwise determined to be innocent. A heart that believes all are frauds is a dangerous land to play in. If you find yourself to be overly skeptic, it's possible that there is a deeper-rooted cause worth investigating and praying about.

Regardless, the cost of accepting counterfeit editions of anything can be great; therefore, it is worth knowing the signs of fraudulent activity to prevent bankrupt spirits. The difference of calling all guilty versus consideration of truth is worth exploring. There is a fine line between the two.

Imagine walking into a busy coffee shop where the cashier scrutinized every bill she received. It would be a mess; the cashier typically would only question those that seem "not quite right." The facts are facts; you've been given an intuition by your father to assist in protecting you. Use it. As with money, if something does not sit right with a person you've recently met or an opportunity, it may be prudent to proceed with caution until positive you're safe.

Most importantly, as anyone who wants to pass you, counterfeit bills would possibly attack when you investigate. A fraud will demand trust before ever giving you any reason to trust them. People who demand trust regardless if you've been given any reason to trust, well, tread lightly.

Be cautious to examine your heart and motives behind investigation as well. It's okay to guard your heart, you should. But isolation rooted in fear is a joyous playground for Satan.

Costly Deception

We would be deceived to believe that counterfeiters would only imitate large bills. But it does happen that large bills are of greatest benefit for deceptive exchanges. The goal is to give a big (false) promise in exchange for something of real value.

If someone or something (a possible spouse, potential business partner, job opportunities, positions change) offers too good to be true exchange, then it's likely of no value to your journey. And if you're being offered such, it may be worth proceeding with caution. It is likely best to use your discernment and scrutiny to be positive this offering is really worth its weight. The exchange that would occur here is no value (their false offering) for what is of great value (you.)

Under the Light

The first action that anyone suspecting fraudulent bills should do is place the bill under the light. This is how you can see if the bill has a telltale strip in it.

As with monetary notes, our first action in checking the legitimacy of someone or something is to place it under our Father's light. Light chases out darkness. Ask God to lead you in truth. Be sure your plans line up with theirs. More importantly does the person or "opportunity" line up with God's will. Is your desire to live in service? But your potential spouse has one plan in life, get rich quick. It may be that you're unequally yoked. (More on that later.)

As you're planning to start a business, is your new possible business partner planning to deceive others or serve money? In opposition to your model of business in the service of God, you cannot serve two gods. And if God has placed a desire in your heart to do something, he will provide the way. Don't fall into the trap of allowing another slave master to take over your life. Allow God to be God over your future, and he will make the way.

Shine the light of prayer over any prospects. God will lead you in truth if you allow him to.

Blurred Lines

Another sign that you're dealing with bogus material is blurred lines. Anyone who received a bill with blurry undefined lines would quickly question the bill's value. Likewise, any time you find yourself dealing with anyone who blurs lines, you've been given a gift. This is the gift to reject worthless currency.

Let's say you have a job that seems like it could be the promise you've been looking for. But as you get past the surface, you notice the company really operates at the expense of ethics.

Or imagine your potential business partner encourages you to intentionally blur lines with your customers and expects you to deceive them into purchases.

If you believe God promised you a marriage and the one you fall for is great but is covertly disrespectful, then that isn't God's promise to you. Instead, it is Satan's plan to prevent you from getting what God promised and keeping you in a stronghold.

What these people really want is a permissive spirit. They want to remove the accountability they are avoiding. But they will do so in a manner that is sneaky but still goes against what you're comfortable with. What Satan really wants with his counterfeit offers is the loss of your faith, and he wants you to question the goodness and honesty of God.

Blurred lines seem easy to recognize, but some people are crafty and may find ways to pull you into their schemes. Don't forget the ramifications of Eve's blurred lines. She thought she could handle the serpent. Now most women can't wait to get to heaven and punch the lady right in her uterus. The best thing to do the minute you see the red flag of a blurred line is to remove yourself from the situation all together. Then you must trust God to bring the true version of what it is you are desiring.

Color Shifting

A bill that is legitimate has color-shifting ink. This ink, when the bill is shifted back and forth, will change colors, but the denomination or value doesn't change.

Many people will adjust to their surroundings as the ground around them shifts. So a person who is on unsteady ground may appear to be changing. Change isn't necessarily bad; it is often a sign of a healthy person. The difference? If a person is a legitimate part of God's plan for you, they show their denomination to be steady when their grounds shift.

This may be a little confusing, so let's clarify. Imagine you've started a business with your longtime friend. They seem to pass other tests for proving their value, they really seem to love God and have shown themselves to pray with you, they quote your favorite scriptures, and so on.

This person, at one time, will be very devoted. However, when sands shift, they seem to take a different stance. Maybe they claim high moral grounds with you. But when they are around others, their behaviors change, their attitudes, and moral stance is different. Then when the partner sees you squirm, they quickly shift back to the person whom you thought you knew.

The truth is, all people can step into the murky messy waters of stupid. But a person who shifts their attitudes regarding honesty, integrity, etc., they're likely counterfeit and don't belong in your promised land. That person is one who will easily drag you down.

If someone is comfortable with deception, whether you participate willingly or not, they will deceive others. The problem with your association with them is it's hard to prove your innocence. Guilt by association is a dangerous land to play in. God will not ask you to associate with deceptive spirits to obtain your promises.

Watermarks

In the monetary world, watermarks are smaller replicas of the face on the bill. They reflect what currency they represent. For instance, if you notice Benjamin Franklin on your bill, you should see exactly the same smaller face to the side of the bill.

God made Adam in his image. True authentic people that really belong on your path, they too should be made in God's image. (All people are, and we shouldn't be legalistic about who God loves, but we must be careful not to tie ourselves to sinking ships.)

Authentic promises should reflect the image of our father. God's promises should bear the fruit of the spirit. Their actions, attitudes, and behaviors should represent God. When you see God shining through them, you my friend may have found the real McCoy.

Focus Scriptures

For there is nothing hidden that will not be disclosed, and nothing concealed that will not be known or brought into the open. (Luke 8:17 NIV)

Then you will know the truth, and the truth will set you free. (John 8:2 NIV)

Do not be misled: "Bad company corrupts good morals." (1 Corinthians 15:33 NIV)

Focus Prayer

Pray that God will reveal counterfeit versions of your promises, that he will lead you in truth, and give you a heart that refuses to accept anything less than his best.

Chapter 7

Equally Yoked Alliances

When my daughter was little, she played on a youth soccer team. As far as winning goes, let's just say her team was lacking. To be transparent, my offspring did nothing to help. She was unsure of any goals in either literal or figurative regards. (She is grown now and jokingly says when it comes to life, not much has changed.) It was entertaining, but I never expected much in the way of seeing my child become the star player. She was only about six years old when she began playing, so she was truly clueless in what the point of the game was. She never touched the ball, just followed the team, and happily ran from one side of the field to the next.

If this were the case for an adult teammate, it wouldn't be quite as cute. But the facts are undeniable. Some aren't working toward any goals whatsoever. It isn't that they're bad people, but they're not the ones you want on your team. If your goal is to make it to any specific promised land, you must have team players that will foster forward motion. Imagine your life's work is dedicated to missions. But imagine being married to a spouse who prevented you from working with the church due to jealousy or codependency. The person doesn't have the same goals you have; therefore, they will not serve with you. But they will also prevent your purpose from ever unfolding in this world. Or if you feel you have a book to write, but those in your life say it can't be done, sad to say, they really don't belong in your corner.

This is a matter of being unequally yoked. Some may see it as a softer form of being unequally yoked, but I'm convinced it is more destructive. A yoke in regards to animals (typically oxen) is a wooden bar that keeps two animals united. The bar fits over their necks and enables them to work better together. Together. Imagine your walk with God as the yoke; it is there to help you to walk united with those you're working with. God offers helpmates to accomplish bigger things than you could ever do alone. But you need to be sure those you allow in your life are equally yoked. This way, you will be enabled to work toward the same purpose in unison. The last thing you need when trying to focus on your goals is an ox who is trying to pull you in the wrong direction...or even off the edge off a cliff.

Safe Alliances

Ally (noun, plural allies), one that is associated with another as a helper, a person or group that provides assistance and support in an ongoing effort, activity, or struggle

Many wartime struggles call for allies. If you're in a battle for your life's purpose to unfold, you will need the proper allies on your team. You need to have those who you can share your vulnerabilities without concern of them exposing those weaknesses or attacking your areas of susceptibility.

A person God will place on your team will be the person who you can share your deep desires along with your wounds and fears. Allies will promote your desires. Additionally they will meet your wounds and fears with encouragement, support, and hopefully with prayer.

Imagine meeting the love of your life (second to God, of course). Your loved one learns of your past wounds, broken places, and greatest fears. This person has two choices regarding your vulnerable truths, expose them and use them as weapons or mend the wounds and protect them from further damage.

Just as allies of war, you must be careful that those who head to your promises are safe allies. Imagine knowing that you're facing warfare and others depend on your coming through for them. Countries who are in alliance with one another have to expose parts of themselves with certainty that their allies won't use that information to wound but instead to help.

I once had a friend who confided in me that she had a dream of being a nurse. What's interesting is that I had known her as a secretary for a while before ever knowing this. I thought she was phenomenal as a secretary and would have always believed she had fit into her purpose had she not told me of a greater dream.

Her ally, her spouse, was actually the one who pushed her further than her sight was willing to take her. She told me how she wanted to go back to school for coding. When she told me this, I was excited for her. I knew just as she was as a secretary, she would be incredible in coding. Yet when her husband heard this, she joked that he "bullied" her into living out her deeper dream.

Her husband was a perfect example of a safe ally. He was willing to support her in her current role. He was willing to support her in her journey to coding. But my friend's husband is a much better ally than one who only supports what he sees; he would support what she wanted but was maybe not comfortable proclaiming.

This is what it truly means in Proverbs 27:17 (NIV), "As iron sharpens iron, so one person sharpens another. These are the allies you want on your team."

Who are your allies? Look around you and ask God for assistance in finding the right kind of allies so that you may truly win the war. Pray God brings allies that will assist you into your promised land.

Focus Scriptures

As iron sharpens iron, so one person sharpens another. (Proverbs 27:17 NIV)

Chapter 8

Pack Your Bags

In earlier chapters, we explored what must be unpacked. It is now known how to spot counterfeits. And you've hopefully learned the beauty of safe allies.

Now it's time to load up the wagon for the journey. But what belongs in your pack? What is beneficial to take with you? What yoke will you take upon you? In Exodus 12:35, the Israelites asked the Egyptians for valuables (gold, silver, and clothing) to take with them on their journey. You will need clothing; you will need to be clothed with the garments of salvation. God has wrapped you with a golden robe of righteousness. You will need to wear the helmet of salvation. You will need to learn how to walk in the identity he assigned to you by proclamation of his word, more on that in a later chapter.

For now, let's get to packing as we have exciting places to be.

Your packing list:

- Submission
- Trust and obedience
- Faith and courage
- Commitment
- Vision
- Patience
- Appreciation
- Staying the course

- Satisfaction with progression
- Blind perseverance
- Focused determination
- Surrender

I know, I know. I've listed blind perseverance on the same packing list with vision and focus. Seems oxymoronic. I'm aware. Just go with it.

Submission to God's Will

I live on the side of a plateau. This means that in order to get to town, I must take a spindly road down the side of a mountain. Every few years or so, heavy rains yield a washed-out road. The joy of such means that in order to go to town, those who live in this area must journey a long way around and down another ridge. Honestly, this is no fun. This detour transforms a ten-minute drive into around a thirty-minute haul. It stinks.

The road department had placed road closure signs at the top of the mountain. However, due to inconvenience, some chose to move the signs and go around them. Because of their rebellion, local officials had to place a barricade in order to protect drivers from falling with the crumbling road. Still yet some persisted. This leads to larger lighted signs and more concrete barriers.

The road may not have appeared to be as dangerous to those desiring to avoid the longer drive. However, what they were unaware of or chose to ignore is that the road closure was due to an unseen problem. The road that was cracked and slightly shifted had weakened ground underneath. It was unstable and dangerous land to play on. One wrong move or a bit too much weight and the entire road could cave in.

The long way around to town, it's actually very pretty in some areas. And it isn't always so bad if one is willing to soak in the beauty.

On your journey, there may be some unexpected detours. And they may seem to cause you to have to take the long way around.

Study the Israelites' journey, and you will find God intentionally led them on a longer journey than seems reasonable.

You may experience the same. God may give you road closures. God may give you signs to show you where you want to go isn't in his will or even safe for you to walk on. Don't try to go around his barricades; he is only protecting you from your fall. Submit to his will. He may have a beautiful road for you to travel.

Trust and Obedience

"I said get out of the boat! I'm serious. Get out. Now." That is how Jesus would talk to me if I were expected to get out of any boat to walk on water. More accurately speaking, I'm doubtful I would ever get on the boat in the first place.

Okay, I'm somewhat hypocritical. I am the same author who wrote about the restrictive nature of comfort zones. I am also the same person admitting that to get me on the boat in the middle of an ocean would be a horribly uncomfortable experience.

Have you read the story of Jonah? (Though I guess it wouldn't have been written this way had Jonah obeyed.) I know what happened to the *Titanic*. I once watched a video where a man was on a ship that sank, he survived in the ship for three days...at the bottom of the ocean. The bottom. Let that "sink" in. Should Jesus ever expect me to get out of any boats to walk on water, it's possible the story would go like this: Jesus would apathetically say, "Fine," as he would have to start sinking the ship.

I would respond with a disgruntled, "Okay, okay. Fine!" Then and likely only then would get out. Sadly, our sinking ship of crisis is sometimes what it takes to get any movement from us at all.

While stepping out of our ships of comfort zones may seem daunting, trusting in God to keep us afloat and obedience to his guidance is all that will prevent you from sinking. You won't always feel comfortable walking on the waters of faith. You will likely feel yourself sinking in the process of your faith journey. But trust will carry you. You will have moments when all you can do is say, "I trust you." Even if you're not fully convinced your words are true, you can say them.

No matter how uncomfortable you are, no matter how scared you become, trust and obedience are like your life vest. Keeping your eyes on God is what it will require to wear the vest of trust and obedience. When you have your eyes on him, you will see it is he who wants your purposes to succeed. When you possess this knowledge, trust and obedience becomes more natural. You will recognize that his instructions (even when they're confusing) are for your good and his purposes.

Has God been prompting you to get out of the boat of your comfort? Has God been showing you ways he wants to use you? Are you obedient enough to do what he asks of you? Trust and obedience is one of the most vital things you could ever pack for the journey ahead.

Faith and Courage
And Willingness to Look Absolutely Nuts

"Our mom is broken. I think we need a new one." Apparently, my daughter believes singing and dancing in a manner that screams, "I'm somewhat insane," makes one "broken." I didn't care who was watching. I was in musical heaven. I have long since left behind the small girl in me that minds, looking absolutely nutso. I like all kinds of bizarre music, but I guess this particular day, my choice genre had my children confused. Honestly, I was more confused by their confusion than they were by my behavior. My behavior was nothing out of my (abnormal) ordinary. Certainly, by now, they would have been used to it.

I'm not afraid to dance in the rain. Spontaneous desires to paint murals on my living room walls bring me no shame. I'm not above loading into my vehicle at any time to head to whatever random place that suits my fancy that very moment. I will burst into song, singing unintelligible words without any real method or warning. I don't even know if what I sing is real words. If I only had a dollar for every time I heard the words *you're not right*, I could find myself on the top list of Forbes richest beings. I don't care how I look, if I'm enjoying the simplicity of life, all is well. I have the beautiful freedom of being comfortably me.

However, Christian existence offers opportunities to look beyond absurd. Seriously, folks just don't get us. Have you ever considered how it felt to be Noah? "Hey, guys, so uh, you're gonna die." What about Abraham? "I know it seems crazy, Sarah, but, we're older than time and making a baby." Mary? "I've never known a man, but yeah, so I'm pregnant." Moses... "Manna will rain from heaven, waters will part, a staff will turn into a snake, and I will be your fearless stuttering leader."

"Yeah, Moses, I am going to need all your sharp items. Let me show you to your rubber room. But I ain't going anywhere with you."

What about you? What crazy belief are you standing on? Do you look at your bank account to bill ratio and think, *There's no way I'll get out of debt, but I know with God I can.* Or *no one in our family has ever started a business, but somehow, I know I will succeed.* Does what you're believing God has spoken into your heart make your family or friends believe you're somehow broken? Has God breathed something deep into the pits of your heart, but those around you don't fully understand your promise?

What God does in our lives and how he moves rarely ever makes sense or looks acceptable to others. You don't need their approval to write a book, go back to school, or become the person you're made to be. You need God's hand over it. You may have to be willing to risk, looking like you've gone berserk.

Your faith will take courage to walk in. And sometimes courage looks strikingly similar to insanity. But faith is the key to unlocking heaven's promises over your life. A dream that doesn't require faith to achieve. Well, is that really a dream worth seeing come to fruition? Have faith, stay courageous, trust God, and look absolutely bonkers! And I dare you to dance in the rain.

Commitment

Even if it means committing to looking nuts, you must do so. A dear loved one was once a participant in a challenge to run daily for thirty days. The eventual plan for all participants was to run a longer distance together as a team.

When my loved one was traveling, he found himself running up and down the sidewalk of a truck stop and in circles around the parking lot of his hotel. He laughed about how silly he must've looked. Naturally, due to my rotten nature, I wanted to heckle him. However, I couldn't. I found his behavior admirable. I knew his behaviors are why he is in fabulous shape. Who could chastise and not make a fool of themselves?

The truth is his parking lot actions spoke louder than my behaviors in the safety of the gym do. I tend to have a real sense of gymtimidation. That's gymtimidation—the sense or feeling of being out of place, more specifically speaking, immensely awkward with the buff kids in the gym.

Not this guy, nope, my beloved was determined. And it didn't matter who was looking or where he was. As a matter of fact, his actions challenged me to stop making excuses and to stop allowing my discomfort to keep me stagnant. When I was later in a meeting, I found myself feeling restless. I wanted to run a bit. All I had was a parking lot and high heels.

Crow, should you have a taste, is best served with salt and a side of humble pie. I had a moment where I considered how I would look, and then I remembered my loved one's physique. It didn't come from stagnancy, lack of commitment, or fear of how others perceive him. Furthermore, time revealed that his perseverance led to his three-man team winning first place in a fifty-mile race. No taunting happened that day, only smiles and cheers.

The things you're committed to doing today, they'll possibly look a little absurd to others. That's okay; those very people may eventually find promptings to take action in their lives by your behaviors. Regardless of other perceptions, your results will only come from full commitment.

Tootsie's Rose
(Vision)

She was somewhat savage, a beast, a real force to be reckoned with. She was eccentric, she was determined, and she didn't let others write her storyline. Opinions of those without proper perspective didn't stand a chance of survival around her. As a visionary of her time, if she proclaimed it, so it would be. She was my hero. Unfortunately, I never met her other than through stories. Her name? Tootsie.

Tootsie was a friend's great-great-aunt. Her title "great-great" was deserved as she was greater than just one minor "great." I'm certain that if I ever knew Tootsie, I would be writing an entire book on her life and hilarious behaviors. It would be a form of unjust neglect not to describe Tootsie's every feature down to the story behind each wrinkle she ever earned. To fail to chronicle her life would be tragedy, as some legends deserve to live forever. From what I know of her, Tootsie's life surely warrants a great southern novel written in her honor.

For today, all I can offer is a simple tribute to Tootsie's unwavering foresight. My friend's dad, who apparently had limited perception (bless his heart), once made a failed attempt to present reality to Tootsie.

"What are you doing with those sticks?" he asked Tootsie.

"They're not sticks, they're roses," she replied.

"Those aren't roses, they're sticks," my friend's father (who shall remain anonymous for his protection) protested.

"They're roses," Tootsie exclaimed, and without explanation, she spat on the sticks and shoved them into the ground.

In time, one of the two participants of this story was proven wrong, and it wasn't Tootsie. Rose bushes began sprouting. I imagine Ms. Feisty pants grinned an all-knowing grin as she had her "I told ya so" moment.

It's rare that radical dreams or actions look appealing to others. It is unlikely that whatever has been breathed into your spirit will make sense to anyone. You may see roses where others can only see sticks. That's okay, spit on the stick and proclaim, "It's a rose."

Later when you reap the fruits of your labor, you'll likely be grinning to yourself saying, "God told me so." You don't need the approval of others, only God's. Start planting.

Patience

"So how long until we leave?" These are words I dread hearing more than most. If I'm off work and planning a day outing, I'm rarely in a hurry. More accurately, I rarely plan ahead, and if I've decided to take an outing or road trip, it is frequently spur of the moment. Regardless of the details behind if the trip is planned or spontaneous, hurrying is my kryptonite. This fact is something that absolutely drives my daughter batty. If you ask me the best way to ruin any spur of the moment trip is to hurry it along. Feeling rushed is just not fun to me. I've spent countless hours rushing about in my line of work. As a mother, I've had to watch the clock more than I ever wanted to. So when I'm off, I refuse to be a slave to time.

My daughter on the other hand, she wants to know when we're leaving, and she really gets fed up with my dawdling. What this conflict usually comes down to is my final answer of "rushing me doesn't increase my speed or change any outcome whatsoever. I'm busy and your protests are counterproductive. Just relax or help me, and I'll tell you when I'm almost finished packing."

Sorry to inform, God isn't in a hurry either, you are. Your persistent heckling will not change his plans or the outcome. You may as well pack some patience into your bag for the trip and be ready to wait. In time, you'll find there is joy in the wait. There is a method to God's timing, and while you're waiting, God is working.

Appreciation

Heaven, help me. Should I ever take this for granted? I thought to myself as I took the final bites of the finale of a seven-course meal. I was finally eating the meal I had booked long in advance. Should I return? My chances of getting back to this restaurant anytime soon were minimal. And I certainly would not have a five-star chef personally visit my table before I returned. So I wanted to savor not just the food but also the moment.

Some things, like my once-in-a-lifetime meal, should never be taken for granted. Yet it happens. Imagine a chef bringing you a delightful loaf of bread; each bite melts in your mouth. Your senses light up. The smell is incredible. The taste is delectable. Sweet hints of heaven's goodness please your tongue as you realize the king of the universe, God himself, prepared this for you. You never had to book appointments months ahead. You only had to wake up, and manna from heaven poured right to the breadbasket on your front porch. These things don't happen. They're not mundane experiences. I can say I've never needed a manna umbrella.

However, after years of their wilderness journey, the Israelites were done with manna. They were ready for their other courses. They murmured and complained regardless of the fact that every morning, they experienced miracles others have never seen.

Miracles are only as good as our appreciation of them. The things we once prayed and thanked God for can begin to feel stagnant when we lose our appreciation for them. Today, I want to challenge you to recognize beauty and resist complacent attitudes toward God's provisions. Take time to savor his love and gifts given to you.

Appreciation on your journey will take you a long way.

Staying the Course

I'm the last person anyone wants to watch TV with. I'll quickly admit this fact. I was once told, "My god mom, if you don't shut up, I'm going to throw my phone at your head."

I quickly become restless, and if the program I'm watching doesn't get my attention or go in the direction I want it to, two things will happen. One, I become mouthy. I'll make fun of every aspect of the show. Or two, I'll give up on it and stop watching the series all together.

This was the case when I watched a show that seemed to become redundant. My friends asked me if I had made it to the same episode as they had.

"No, I gave up on it. It was the same thing over and over again."

"I know, but pick it back up! It gets so good!" I did. And they were right. I would have missed a great program if I gave in to my incessant ADD.

If your chapter of life that you're in seems a bit redundant or unending, give it time. You have the best author writing your story.

Satisfaction with Progress

Three large stone markers stand on a field in the outer banks. Each stone represents the distance that the Wright brothers made with their first flights. The first two weren't very far at all. The third stone? Distance was gained!

One could only imagine how the brothers felt with each flight. I suspect elated would sufficiently describe their feelings. But what if they decided that since they didn't make it as far as they wanted during their first flight, they would call it quits? Would we fly today? Would we know modern-day aviation to be that of a little boy's fancy?

Just because you don't fly on the first attempt doesn't mean you won't. Everything you learn in the process may even lead to others flying higher than ever expected. You will have to learn how to be as excited with your progress as you are about your destination.

It has been said that Thomas Edison made a thousand light bulbs before one was actually successful. Again, what if he quit when things didn't go his way?

Just because your first attempt at starting a business was unsuccessful, it doesn't mean the next flight won't take off entirely. No one ever expects a baby to walk without falling on their first steps. It isn't a reasonable expectation. Set reasonable expectations for yourself, and learn how to be satisfied with progress.

Who knows how high you'll fly!

Blind Perseverance

One weekend, while my daughter was home from college, we decided to go for an afternoon hike. The trail we went to wasn't well marked. Nor was it frequently traveled. The proof was in the evidence. It had many areas that weren't as cleared as those paths that are frequented by many travelers. We had limbs to dodge, we had to climb over fallen trees, and we only hoped we were headed in the general direction of the falls.

It was hard to tell if we were in the right area at all. There weren't any other travelers to ask if we were headed in the right direction. It was mostly guesswork. The truth is the trail was generally lacking in scenery. Period. Finally, we decided to turn back. I really had no desire to become a news story of missing persons.

As we left, my daughter went ahead with our dogs. I stayed behind to wander and pray a little. Eventually a man who must have been the only other man around at the time walked up behind me.

So I asked, "Did you find a waterfall?"

He replied, "Yes, as a matter of fact, it wasn't far from where I first walked up on you. It's huge and beautiful. You should consider going back."

I didn't because my daughter was pretty far ahead by this point. But I had a feeling that had I persisted, we wouldn't have missed out.

Our paths will often feel like this. That's because if you're seeking growth, you are on a path less traveled. So it's hard to tell if you're traveling in the right direction at all. There won't necessarily be trail markings to let you know you are on the right path. You'll have obstacles like those fallen trees and overgrown stray branches. But you mustn't turn back.

So the path is lackluster. Your journey will occasionally require you to soak in the beauty of a moment. But sometimes it is more important that you blindly persist without knowing if your directional compass is correct or not. Do you really want to miss out on what lies ahead if the scenery is something beautiful?

Focus

Some friends of mine were once talking about a television program they liked. One admitted they had stopped watching due to the fact that the show had lost focus. "They all stopped fighting zombies and just started fighting one another. That's when I lost interest."

Life can be very similar to what my friends were talking about. We often lose our focus on which battles we should be fighting. This is actually a war tactic of Satan. He wants us too distracted to complete God's plans. So he will throw you curveballs. I can attest to this on a very personal level.

In writing this book, every time I would think I was nearing completion and ready to submit it to publishers, life put another wrench in my gears. I've dealt with very emergent problems to minor distractions along the way. I faced unmentionable battles and the financial and the stressful ramifications of said battles, then came my father's diagnosis of a rare terminal illness, the questions, "Will my kids and myself have this disease?" I suffered through the loss of my best friend, then my grandmother passed away soon after, I had a job change, the coronavirus pandemic occurred. Name it, it happened. I had adversity in my workplace that I didn't see coming, and it hurt deeply. If that wasn't enough, I was diagnosed with stage three incurable cancer and started chemo. I honestly thought I would lose my marbles.

With each challenge, the book was placed on the back burner. With each battle, I felt that I was fighting the most important thing I could at the moment. But I began to doubt that God wanted me to publish at all. And when COVID struck, I questioned if the book was even relevant anymore. How could I encourage people to chase victory when it seemed the world was crashing and burning? I felt like not only a fraud but didn't know which battle was most important anymore. "What do I fight?"

It is easy for us to lose focus and start battling fights that aren't ours to fight. You have somewhere you need to be. And there will be a lot of distracting fights for you to battle. They're not all the battles you're supposed to fight though. Don't get distracted by things that don't matter. Fight for what you're attempting to do and don't waste energy on other problems.

Obviously, you will have some real problems present themselves. I won't pretend it won't happen. Just as I faced more than the lion's share, you may have some things that you cannot ignore. All you can do in these situations is do your best and let God do the rest. Focus your eyes on him and let him help you battle it out.

Surrender

It is somewhat oxymoronic that I would write anything about surrender. It isn't my strong point. Surrender is, however, something I'm learning is beneficial for my advancement.

To start, let's define "surrender," it means cease resistance to an enemy or opponent and submit to their authority. It's interesting to consider that God wants us to even need to surrender. As it says above, cease resistance.

Now I'm the first to admit, to stop resisting is tough. I would prefer to have some control in my life. But to further dissect the word *surrender*, it gets more threatening to oneself because it says cease resistance to an enemy. That's where this becomes confusing. Because deep down, we don't want to see God as an enemy, but we often will turn him into our opposition by resisting what he desires of us.

Though hard to explain, it is true. I want you to stop for a moment and think of whatever battles you may be facing. Is part of that battle with God over his will? I want to ask you this, is God your enemy? Does God in his love and wisdom desire to harm you?

God is not your enemy. He is a father who desires to help you with whatever it is you're facing. But you will have to surrender to his purposes and plans. Stop resisting his will.

No matter how hard it is, it is necessary to surrender to God if you desire a life in promise.

Though I am not the best to advise how to do so, I have admitted, I'm not very good at letting go, and I can offer prayer.

Today, while reading this, I pray you will take a moment to pray for surrender. "Not my will but yours be done." I also believe sometimes we need help doing so. So I think this fact should guide your prayers. It's okay to admit, "God, I don't want this. And I don't even know how to be submissive to your will. Help me do this."

There really is power in letting go and letting God have control because it is in his control that great things can be done.

Chapter 9

The Wilderness

Are We There Yet?

A gentle breeze on my face and the aroma of pine needles delighted my senses. The sound of birds singing, frogs croaking, and the crunch of the path under my bicycle tires reminded me of the joy of crossing another item off my bucket list. Ahh!

The Virginia creeper! I'm here. I'm really here! I thought. And the words began to flow freely, "We're guaranteed nothing. Beauty is to be savored. God gave us an incredible land to explore. Life is too short to spend it too afraid to live, truly live. Moments are fleeting, and life isn't worth wasting listening to music you don't love in the company of hateful people and not crossing items off of your bucket list. Get out there and live, really live. And when you're done, until you're done, keep adding more items to the list and do them!"

My wanderlust attitude toward the Virginia creeper was in full swing. I took pictures; I smiled my best Snow White smile as I watched strangers enjoy the trail's beauty. I closed my eyes to just breathe, really breathe in all God's land has to offer.

"What a beauty this is. Thank you, God, for this opportunity! Thank you, Lord, for this beauty! My heart feels full. Your goodness is astounding, and your love for me is overwhelming."

Then came a new me. At about mile fourteen, I found out the hard way I have VCMPD, Virginia creeper multiple personality disorder. My joyful attitude had given its retirement notice and worked out its final notice. The retirement party was over, and the aftermath mess was all I had to look at. The beautiful soul that graced the beginning of the trail had somehow been left behind. The poor girl likely cried as she was left alone on mile tenish and watched me fade into the distance. Or maybe not, the happy nature nut is likely still out there somewhere enjoying the scenery.

But the inner me that I was left to ride the trail with, what a troll. She wasn't sure she was even on the correct trail anymore. She questioned her sense of direction; she questioned her existence. She wasn't satisfied with the journey that she had to take alone; she wished she had at least one friend to wander with. All the while that sinister gal likely couldn't keep friends as she despised the gusto other bikers still possessed. "Enjoy the trail!" Don't tell me what to do, random passerby! Get me off this trail. My seat is hurting…my seat. Why did I pack such a heavy pack? Next time, I'll travel with a lighter load so this won't be so hard. Next time? I'm just not sure there will be a next time.

Would it be abuse of emergency services to call for assistance off the trail? Maybe, but I was convinced I would need the Jaws of Life to peel my flesh off my bicycle. The words of the shuttle service employee rang in my mind, "I promise you'll love it. You'll be back." Ha. Who was he to tell me how to feel about this path? Love it? I may set it on fire. Be back? Not even.

Promises are no different. With indescribable enthusiasm, we saddle up our camels excited for the road ahead. When God first whispers our desires into our hearts, our souls become ablaze with energy. But when the road gets bumpy and our comfort eludes us, when we feel the sting of having to travel alone and wish we had a friend to go with, it's easy to want off the path immediately.

"Nine-one-one, what's your emergency?"

"I need the Jaws of Life out here in the wilderness, I'm uncomfortable. No, I'm exhausted. I'm alone. I was certain I would have arrived by now. I am not certain if I'm on the right path. And I've made the mistake of thinking I would enjoy this trail."

Imagine you've obeyed God; you know he has told you to take steps of faith and journey away from your captors. You recognized the starvation for something better within you and became determined to feed your hunger for a better life. You decided to fight back. You left what would hinder your walk with God. You invited those who were invested in progress to journey with you. You watched as God washed away what doesn't belong on the path. You believed life was going to look better. Yet as you unpack your last can of beans and laid down for the night, another night in the wilderness, tired and weary. "Why did I come out here? At least when I was a captive, I had food, comforts of modern-day conveniences, but now, it's me, and it's this rock I'm using as a pillow. The food has run out worse, yet my belief in what I set out to do has dried up."

Sound familiar? I think that is how the Israelites felt. But what they failed to see is that the wilderness is where their faith muscles were being worked out. Without the lack they experienced in the wilderness, they wouldn't have known about manna being poured from heaven.

God does so much behind the scenes. But those lacking moments, the wilderness, the seasons of drought are when God is preparing you for the weight of Promised Land victory. You're out here now, here in the land of uncertainty. You're in the wilderness. But why? You may have a lot to learn before you can withstand the promises of God. One of the most important things you need to know is who God is. You need to know how he provides, and you need to be so strong in your faith that you can bear the weight of what lies ahead without questioning your father's abilities. Therefore, while you're out here, take the time to learn. The wilderness is a classroom. And the classroom has purpose.

My youngest has come home from school night after night, wanting electronic time. I don't mind a little time, but I began noticing he was ignoring his responsibilities. So I had to tell him, get your homework done, and then you can have electronic time. I enjoy watching him grow and learn, just as God enjoys watching our growth. But growth doesn't occur without a little homework, and sometimes the homework has to come before the reward of what we want.

This season you feel you're stuck in honey, it's only for your benefit and growth. When you're done with your homework, God will give his promises.

Over the next chapter, we will explore the many purposes of wilderness seasons. The wilderness is similar to a woman's womb or a butterfly cocoon. It is a place of protection, a place for provision, and a place that provides growth until viability is possible. Don't despair. Your wilderness may be a place you dread, but God will show you the beauty of every lesson. When you're finished, you will come out of your cocoon like a beautiful butterfly, better than you were before.

I'll admit I did love the Virginia creeper. And I will be back, likely several times and in all seasons. In time, when you're finished with your wilderness, you too may find you're thankful for the long journey you've tracked.

The Cocoon

I was pleased watching my four-year-old son playing with his friend. It was cute that he wanted his "best friend" to go down the slide with him. Listening to my son giggle when his friend tickled him was precious. My boy and his friend were chums of the most innocent and loving nature. Therefore, I was pretty agreeable to allowing them to do whatever my child requested. That is until the little man asked me if I could microwave his friend.

His friend was a caterpillar. I'm no expert on butterflies, but I'm near certain that there is no rushing their transformation by zapping them. That transformation can only come from the work that is done in a cocoon.

On faith journeys, we often want to have quick fixes. We want to buy a book, *Seven Ways to Get out of your Wilderness Season*, and be done with the struggle. However, the harsh reality of a wilderness season is that there's no rushing it. Despite this fact, wilderness seasons have a purpose, that is, to transform you into something beautiful. Additionally, speaking a cocoon is protective to the transformation of the caterpillar so is your wilderness season. When you do come out, you'll come out better.

So let's not rush anything. Let's not look for a microwaved transformation. Instead, let's embrace all the wilderness has to offer as we proceed over the next chapter. Let's take some time to transform.

Protection in the Desert

It isn't widely known that during WWII, artwork was hidden in a secret place in the Biltmore house. The art was almost hidden in plain sight, yet no one knew it was there. America had learned that Nazis were stealing art, and some became concerned that American art would likely be no different if the Germans invaded America.

With this concerning knowledge, Mr. David Finley (the National Gallery of Art's director) called on Edith Vanderbilt for assistance with hiding national treasures until the war was over. The artwork was brought by train overnight to the Biltmore home and stored behind curtains in a room that people were unaware existed. The room is on the main floor and is part of today's tours. However, at the time the art was hidden, draperies covered the then unfinished room and disguised the room as windows. No one ever knew the art was there.

You've learned your identity is that of a masterpiece created by God. Yet have you found yourself to be unsure as to why you're passed over and so many are unaware of the potential you possess? Your promise was spoken to your heart, and yet as you try to walk in purpose, many just pass you by. Why? What gives?

What you may fail to see is that God is like those who protected artwork during WWII. He knows you're valuable, but he also has the ability to see what you can't. He knows that not all people you encounter have your best interest at heart nor will those people treat you with the care that his works deserve. Some are like Nazis who will steal your identity and destroy the beauty you are. So he hides you in plain sight with drapes over others eyes until it is safe for your reveal.

Ruth, if you're unfamiliar, was a widow who found herself in a period of transition unrelenting. She was left in a season of spiritual drought. She had to glean from the fields of Boaz. When Boaz saw her, he did two things. First, he told his employees to provide for Ruth. He made sure extra grain was left behind for Ruth to gather. Secondly, Boaz told Ruth she should only glean in the confines of his fields, as she may find herself in harm's way otherwise. Boaz told his workers not to lay a hand on her.

While you may not be where you want to be, God may be keeping you in this place to protect you. It's likely he knows what is in the fields of others. He has seen how other employers treat their employees. The doors you so desperately pray will open. He may hold tightly shut to keep you from facing bosses who will do you wrong. He may be protecting you from returning to a life of slavery. He also may see that where you currently stand (even if it doesn't feel like it) is providing more than you could on your own.

While you're here in the wilderness, why not just enjoy it? Soak in the scenery. Recognize like the Virginia creeper didn't become shorter because I was exhausted, your seasons won't change due to your desires or fatigue. Why not just take the time to treat this season as a classroom and let God speak to you, show you who he is and what he desires from you.

Be Still

Living in the sticks has its perks. I am rarely bothered. Most of my neighbors have been neighbors for the majority of my life. I feel pretty safe with them. They're good people. I can enjoy nature's beauty day in and day out. However, on occasion, my peaceful scene is interrupted by uninvited guests.

I've had a bat get into my home. Spiders, mice, and bears, oh my! Okay, no bears. But you get the point. With the occurrence of so many animals breaking in and our inability to deny strays, we often joke that our home is a modern-day Noah's ark.

I was once studying on my living room couch when a copper-head made its way toward me. The large med surg book I was reading became a projectile as I threw it at the snake, killing it instantly. My son was small at the time, so he innocently told so many his mom killed a snake with the Bible. *Cough, cough.* I'm a savage beast. It was cute, so I let the story stick. Isn't that what we're supposed to do? Kill a serpent with our word anyway?

When we had another copperhead on our front porch around a year ago, my daughter (now grown) yelled, "Don't move! I'll get the Bible!" I think I've raised them right.

More recently, I was enjoying a long bath when I heard a scurrying noise. I looked up to see I had a new friend. A lizard had made its way in as it was certain that I would sign a roommate agreement, and all would be well. I wasn't horribly opposed to the little guy. So I left him to roam, and I headed to town. Later that evening, I had been pulling up carpets and doing some dirty work, so I wanted a shower. When I came back to the bathroom, I found the little man had fallen into the bathtub.

I grabbed a dustpan and a soft hanger to nudge him into the pan. He wasn't interested in my eviction notice. He fought and fought against my directions.

"Stop it!" I said. "I'm only trying to put you where you're safe. You'll drown here, and the dogs will eat you!"

He continued to wrestle. In his attempts to get away from me, I noticed one of his legs were flaccid. I am certain his fall had broken it. I was quickly reminded of Jacob and his wrestling with the angel of the Lord.

Is it possible that like this lizard who was safer outside and had more provisions of bugs there, we are safer in the wilderness? The problem is that like the lizard resisting me and Jacob fighting the angel, we often resist what God is doing and fight him tooth and nail. The last thing I want is to be like either with a broken leg. Don't wait till God has to break you to relax and be still. Let him do the work of placing you where you belong.

Later this same day, I watched a video of a man carrying a washed-up dolphin back to ocean water. God is no different than the man in this video. He picks us up, he doesn't scold us or ask us why we're not where we belong, and he simply places us where we are safe.

Then like the man in the video, he watches us to make sure we swim off safely to where we should be. (Deeper waters.)

The difference between the lizard and the dolphin though is that the dolphin didn't resist what the man was doing. The dolphin only trusted and was *still* while the man carried him safely home.

Your wilderness experience may drive you nuts and feel like you're just not where you belong. However, this is a period where you must learn to be still and know that he is God. He will carry you to the best environment for your survival. You must only be still.

Miraculous Wilderness Lessons of Provision

Jesus's first miracle was when he turned water into wine. First known miracle that is. We all know the scene, a wedding where wine ran out, and the family of the couple was to become a laughing stock. Gasp! The shame! Mary turned to Jesus and told him to do something.

Jesus's answer, "Woman, what matter of this is mine?"

I have to admit I find his response to be comical. His words sound like a classic mother and child conversation. But what I want to really point out is Mary didn't hesitate to ask for help from her son.

Would you? Would you ask your child to concern himself with matters such as wine? A wedding is where mothers may teach their children about etiquette if they bring them at all. However, this is where Mary started showing the world about the Jesus she knew. She had spent years with him and knew his capabilities. His birth alone was a miracle she knew from day one who he was. So she didn't bat an eye with her request.

I'm convinced she saw more miracles than were ever recorded prior to "this first miracle." So miracles to her were likely a standard part of her day. I'm not saying she expected magic Jesus, but I do suspect she had to rely on the power of God to come through her child much sooner than we know of.

The wilderness is a place where we should be spending time in Jesus's presence. It is where we learn about his character. We learn about his ability to perform miracles in seasons of brokenness and necessity. As we learn provisions from God are not always as we expect. (I doubt the Israelites expected to get their dinner in the form of a rain sandwich.) However, this is how we learn not to question his ability.

When Jesus performed this wedding miracle, he asked for gathering of water, and he has done the rest. What if Jesus is only asking you to bring what you do have, and he will bring the miracle? What if like Mary showing the world who her son was and what he was capable of, when you come out of your wilderness, you too show the world what Jesus is capable of?

Wilderness Healing

Why? Why, I ask, did ol' Humpty Dumpty have to fall? Why was he on a wall in the first place? Was the height of his wall representative of his ego? Was Humpty a man who dabbled in heights he could not bear the weight of? Is it that he couldn't handle what he was called to because he was too fragile? Some believe Humpty was actually representative of real people, colonies, and real life falls from grace.

For all intents and purposes, today Humpty will be an illustration of brokenness. When one falls, when a person becomes broken, there is a tendency to run to all the king's horses and all the king's men expecting them to put our Humpty spirits together again. We take our pain and brokenness to relationships, expecting that another person have any ability to heal these wounds.

The problem is we don't take our problems to the king. Expecting healing from any source other than God is similar to expecting artificial plants to provide oxygen. Wilderness seasons are where we can take all our brokenness for repair. Forget the king's horses. Forget the king's men. Bring your trial to the king to be put back together again.

No matter how necessary the wilderness of your life may be, you may find yourself to be like Humpty, broken and wondering if you'll ever be whole again. Some wounds take time to fully heal. Some wounds take extensive measures to bring healing. As a nurse,

I've seen wounds that took only a few moments or hours to form, take years to heal. I've witnessed physicians reopen wounds and cut away dead tissue from wounds. I have placed more solutions and ointments on wounds than I could ever imagine giving account to.

I cannot think of many times when patients didn't have some fear of the pain they faced with wound care. With the deeper wounds, I found many who cringed at the work it took to clean and debride these wounds. But the unfortunate truth is, whatever unhealthy tissue was left behind could only leave the patient with wounds that would likely become infected and would reopen and could cause greater and very serious messes. The only way to deal with any wound is to truly deal with it!

None of us likes pain. I know I am the one who wants to avoid pain. However, there have been moments in my life that pain has been something I've been thankful for. Some pains we face are resuscitative in nature.

Purposed Pain

One late September night, I was awakened by a severe headache, sore throat, and neck pain. I had noticed a rash on my legs, but my youngest child was diagnosed with strep throat the day before. I gave little thought to my symptoms as I suspected I likely had strep as well. I took some medication, went to bed, and thought that if all persisted, I would go to the doctor on Monday.

I worked soon after and noticed my symptoms kept getting worse, and I felt terrible. I was nauseous, had a fever, and was overall extremely tired. Interestingly what finally got my attention was the fact that I began having severe joint pain. I then remembered that I had a tick bite not long before that. I went to see a doctor, thinking maybe I had contracted Lyme disease. The physician did labs, and to both of our surprise, he diagnosed me with Rocky Mountain spotted fever. Without treatment, RMSF is lethal.

I ignored so many symptoms, thinking, *I'll go to the doctor soon.* But the truth is, deep down, I was hoping all my symptoms would subside, and I could avoid seeing a physician. If I had not experienced such strong pain, dramatic sting, I may have perished.

There is pain associated with wilderness seasons. Stepping away from any season will prove to have challenges and heartache associated. But there is a purpose for pain. Pain is intended to show us that something is wrong. Pain has a purpose to get us to fix whatever is off.

Don't be afraid to experience pain. It may be that this is your cue to take your wounds to the great healer. It may be that like those who have great deep physical wounds, you have wounds that God has to get deeper into to fully heal. Some have to have debridement that goes deep down to find healthy tissue to work with. God may be working to get deep into your business to get to the places that were healthy before infection set in. If you find you're hurting and don't appreciate the wounds you feel so strongly, bring your wounds to the greater physician. It may take time but the healing is worth it.

The cost of leaving wounds unmended may be greater than the pain you are avoiding. Eventually as with physical wounds, if infected our spirits will break open and spill out all the nastiness that was left untreated inside. Let God use this season of wilderness to heal you.

The healing purpose of the wilderness is too great to ignore. Without healing, one will latch onto any one thing person or opportunity for happiness. (No matter how counterfeit they know the "thing" to be.) The problem is, this behavior will lead the person right back to the cycle of enslaved living. A person who refuses to acknowledge the pains of their enslavement and confront them face-to-face will travel around the same painful Mountain time and time again.

Remember the lady at the well. She had married several men and was living with another one. I can't assign thoughts, feelings, or beliefs to what it was that made her want to marry repeatedly yet never find satisfaction. But I can speculate that she was traveling around the same mountain over and over because she never took the time to heal what was originally broken. It was only when she met Jesus that a stronghold was broken.

If God allows you to be in a wilderness season, the beauty of the season is that God can use this season to heal all the wounds accrued from seasons of slavery. This season of wilderness may be intended to bring you to his healing well waters and prevent you from continuing around the same mountains over and over and over…

It isn't easy to be in a season of waiting. It's hard to understand why God would leave us to watch others who make it to their promises while we feel we're laying lame at the gate of beauty. Imagine being the man who was laying at the gate, watching others walk around unappreciative of the blessings they had. He had to watch daily as others had what he likely wanted. The encounter of healing he received is what helped him to make it through his gate. I suspect when he did make it through the gate, he appreciated the beauty of the other side much more than his cohorts that probably took beauty for granted.

When God leaves you in the wilderness, it is to help heal you enough so that when you do make it to the Promised Land, like the lame man, you're actually able to walk in purpose. Without healing in the wilderness, it is possible the weight of the Promised Land will leave you unable to cope and handle operate in purpose. Healing is a vital part of surviving any enslaved season. I hope though that after such a season, you'll appreciate the beauty of victory that much more when it does occur. And I hope that you'll walk through your beautiful gates to your promises.

The Tail End

The "Tail of the Dragon" is a winding section of US 129 that leads from Tennessee to North Carolina. This particular section of the road is well known to motorcyclists and sports car enthusiasts. The twisty curves that hug the mountain provide the perfect opportunity for those in need of a good ol' joyride.

I recently traveled this road myself in my sporty minivan. On my journey, I noticed a gaggle of Mazda convertibles. I wanted to stop to request membership to their cool kid crew. However, I'm uncertain of my welcome to their club. Minivans need not apply.

Onward I traveled as the solo member to my dream team gang. I did dabble in the occasional whispering, "zoom, zoom," with each pass-erby. However, I dawdled my way down the mountainside in awe of the glorious wonder that is nature.

They're missing it, I thought to myself. *All the beauty that this world has to offer, and they're missing it.* Then arrived my obligatory nurse's thought process, *People who rush on this road don't always make it out alive people, slow your roll.* A thought I had to dismiss so I wouldn't miss my opportunity to admire nature's offerings.

Despite my concerns, the Mazda mentality seemingly had only one focus, enjoying their machinery's ability to travel at light-ning-fast speeds around curve after curve. Who could blame them? Their behavior reeked of youthfulness.

Still, from my perspective, it appeared they missed the greatest part, the absolute eye candy that was before them. With each twist, a new painting was offered for admiration. Fog steamed off the water. The sunset peeking over the mountains, its light dancing through the trees offered illusions of grandeur. Yet these Mazda cats zoomed on.

Trapped in a wilderness season is hard. We all want to see how fast we can make it out and the "joyride" to be a distant memory. Unfortunately, some seasons cannot be avoided or rushed.

What if? What if you make a choice as you travel on your road? Possibly a single traveler in an uncool mom bus to enjoy the scenery that is around every corner until God opens the doors for the next season?

You may be at the tail end of this season; you may still be at the beginning. Regardless of your position, you have a choice, savor the flavor, or miss what others don't even know is there. Even the wil-derness has beauty to be admired. Rush through it? That's risky. You may not even make it out alive.

Focus Scriptures

"But I will restore you to health and heal
your wounds," declares the Lord, "because you

are called an outcast, Zion for whom no one cares." (Jeremiah 30:17 NIV)

Let us not become weary in doing good, for at the proper time we will reap a harvest if we do not give up. (Galatians 6:9 NIV)

Chapter 10

Dam Life Is Hard

A dammed life (feeling as if flow is prohibited) is hard. Stagnant water stinks, and if you take time to observe any reservoir, you'll notice the debris that settles can be considerably unattractive. Feeling stagnant yields feelings of frustration, and it ain't pretty. But how can you create flow? Truthfully, you may not have the doors of life open unless it's by God's design. Sometimes the only way to see flow at all is to take it by storm.

In two thousand and seventeen, Norris Dam in Tennessee opened for the first time in years. The flow of water from the dam created a calming effect, and many East Tennesseans came to the shorelines to watch. But why after so many years did they finally open up the gates? Storms. Rainfall. And lots of it.

Parts of our destiny can only be broken free by the storms of life. Storms are how God creates flow. Admit it, the flow of a stream is beautiful. Though you may look at stormy situations with disdain, God sees them with different eyes. Storms are promptings that reveal purpose. And storms are part of what will break you free from the wilderness. Storms can be scary, but they create and often illuminate God's plan. Though you may not see it, God will use the details of your storms in more ways than you ever expect. Sometimes your only job is to watch how he works, and then let him reveal purpose.

God knows how to break what is in you free in order to create new growth. In fire-prone regions, some seeds can only grow after a forest fire. These particular trees have seeds that are enclosed with a protective layer. Until fires burn this coating off of the seed, the seed will always be dormant.

Furthermore, if you travel to areas where fires occur more frequently, you will notice only certain trees exist at higher altitudes. This is because only some trees have the ability to survive these fires. Lastly, some trees in these regions have thicker (adaptive) barks to protect them.

God knows two things about you; some seeds that lay dormant in your soul can only birth destiny by trial (our fires). God also knows that the places he is taking you are of higher altitude. If you're going to survive, God will need to help you adapt to the challenges of higher living. You'll need "thicker skin" (bark) for where he is planning to take you.

Therefore, God will allow trials that feel that they will all but take you out. He is only seeking to help you withstand greater purpose.

Stormy Weather

A few years ago, my son was sleeping over at my parents' house. A large storm blew in, and with its gusty wind, the storm brought on a mess none of us saw coming. With powerful force, a large tree behind my parents' home came crashing down right into my parents' home.

The tree, the roof, and the ceiling were all laying on my son. Naturally, he was very shaken. However, other than his anxiety, nothing on him was harmed. I know God protected him. I know I witnessed a miracle when I saw my son alive and without injury after that. This miracle alone was enough. The story could have ended there. The follow-up work God created from this storm that was just delicious icing on the cake.

My parents and family have had many financial obstacles. My parents' home was paid off, but they didn't have insurance. The truth is, the home already needed some work we couldn't afford to do.

Financially speaking, we were left scratching our heads. How would we ever repair what damage was done?

While at work the day after the storm, I was tearful questioning what it would take to cash out some of my retirement funds. I am a single mother. My funds are limited, and I was unsure of any chance I may have to help them. I was barely surviving from the ruins of my personal financial storms. Could they live with me in the meantime? The questions swarmed through my mind leaving me with no true answers, only an abundance of concerns.

My dad had been very ill, unable to walk more than a few feet without becoming short of breath. My brother was facing his storms, and his abilities to help were limited. It seemed we had greater restraints than we had a chance.

Even with the money for supplies, how would we rebuild? I didn't have much in the way of answers, but I did know one thing, I had God. So I prayed, "God, I just don't know how we will do this. It looks like we can't. You have ways where we have none. We really need your help this time. I pray God not only do you help us, but you also make yourself visible to many in the process. Let my parents see you in this. Let others see you." And he did.

I called my dad and told him I would find a way. Dad was crying. He told me that one of my brother's childhood friends had shown up while dad was standing in the yard, crying.

"You practically raised me. I'm not going to let you get wet."

These beautiful friends, friends I consider to be my brothers, all began showing up. They worked diligently to repair the gaping hole that was over my parents' living room, dining room, and kitchen.

While they worked, the pastor from our church arrived. He let my family know they weren't facing anything alone. He brought everyone biscuits, and he visited with my father. Later that evening, as one of the guys were cleaning up, he stopped me to tell me about something the pastor had said.

He was so excited about his encounter with our pastor. What was so significant about this is that this same man had been on the spiritual fence and questioning God's love and the extent of his forgiveness. Little did the pastor know, this person had only ever witnessed harsh criticisms and legalistic form of church. Now he knew the Jesus's side of the true church. While one of these adoptive brothers was there showing my family love, he found out what love from a church looks like. A seed was planted.

The next day, I returned to work still distracted by the concerns over my family's home. I was a little late to a meeting. When I walked in, there was only one chair left to park in. I sat down, and my manager began, "Today I want to do something a little differently. I want us all to go around the room and tell just one thing we're thankful for." Lucky me, my tardiness led to my story being the last. To this day, I'm unsure what came over me, other than the Holy Spirit. I began a purge of tears and tales. I told how thankful I was that in his sovereignty; God had spared my child even when he didn't spare his own. I told of the church's goodness and our pastor's love. I told how my father was seeing firsthand how much God cared for his needs and provided. I was oblivious to much other than the miracles God was performing and the joy of my grateful heart.

When the meeting ended, a friend pulled me aside.

"Wait, I want to tell you something. Did you notice [anonymous cohort] while you were talking?"

I hadn't, but it occurred to me that I had just given account to God's goodness to a man I never knew how to address God with. I had heard this particular person report his atheist beliefs. My friend and I had been praying for him for a while. My friend told me that the entire time I was talking, he was intently listening and nodding his head. Another seed was planted.

When I returned to church the following Sunday, I told the church how thankful our family was. I told how their giving had affected more than just the immediate receivers of their blessings. I told them that like older siblings who give to younger ones, they had shown their spiritual siblings the beauty of their first fruits. They showed others how their generosity had a ripple effect we would likely never know the full extent of.

After church, one of the church members came to me and said, "Thank you for sharing that. I had no idea how much that particular ministry helped others. I've really been wondering where I should put my tithing. I am going to start giving more to this fund." Several seeds were planted.

After the shock of such an event, my son began having some anxieties related to storms. He became an avid weather watcher. Now he can't learn enough about weather patterns. This is his new passion. He is sixteen at present. He is researching schools for meteorology. Seeds were planted in him.

As for my parent's home, well, those brothers often remind me of the men who lowered their friends down to Jesus through a roof. They weren't satisfied watching their loved ones suffer. They repaired my parents' home to better conditions than it has been in years. Seeds grew beyond what we could've ever imagined. As for me, I gained faith I never had before.

It seems that God used a terrible situation for his glory. With the falling of one tree came the planting of many seeds that will grow tall and mighty. While storms bring turmoil, they also water for the seeds of destiny. They bring what it takes to open a dam. If you're facing a storm, it may be the exact wind that brings a shift to your situation. This may be what God uses to show others you've prayed for who he is. This may be what sparks an interest in you or those you love to become what they're intended to be. Storms and fires bring collateral damage, no doubt. But it is the hidden treasures. I implore you to recognize them. Look for his hand. Look for the seeds.

After the Flood

Have you ever wondered how long it took Noah to clean up the mess after the flood? Did he open the doors to the ark and say, "I told ya so! Maybe next time, you will listen to me." Then after seeing the rainbow, did he say, "Oh wait, I guess there won't be a next time. Maybe you should have paid attention!" Did Noah feel distressed that he was effectively left with the aftermath of a flood that had nothing to do with his behavior? Did he have survivor's guilt? Or did he have moments where he wondered if he did something wrong that he had to be the one to build the ark or survive a flood?

When left in a flood, be it finances, relationship loss, or really any trial, it is so tempting to feel anger, especially for what one has to face due to someone else's behavior. It is also easy to feel like storms and trials are due to the wrongdoing of the person facing them. However, floods, storms, and trials are often reflections of what a person has done right. It is a sign that God trusts them with the trial. Gee, thanks God.

Genesis 6:9 says that Noah was a righteous and blameless man, who lived in fellowship with God. In Job 1, Job was described as blameless a man of complete integrity. Some translations say he was God's beloved. What about Jesus? What did he do to deserve the crucifixion? The trial one faces isn't about the storm but instead about what God wants to do with the storm. And a journey toward a promised land will have trials. Just remember though you don't necessarily deserve what you're going through. These trials are formative moments. God can use them for incredible transformation in you. He can use them for his glory.

At War for Purpose

A beautiful home in Franklin, Tennessee, stands to remind us that our trials are not always reflective of something that we deserved. The Lotz home museum is the perfect representation that trials. In this case, war may come knocking literally or figuratively at the doors of the innocent. The Lotz family's story also shows us that while rebuilding may be hard and take some time after tragedy occurs, it is possible.

The Lotz family was a family of German immigrants who were celebrating the birthday of their child, Matilda, one day only to have a civil war battle happening in their front lawn the next day. The family was forced to leave their home. Fleeing meant running between gunfire in a desperate attempt to make it to safety. The family wasn't American; they had no interest in the battle. They did not own slaves. They. Were. Innocent. However innocent they may have been, the Lotz family was left with the aftermath of an incredibly damaged home, no money for repairs, and no food.

The family had to live in the basement of the home while the father rebuilt makeshift floors using only readily available supplies he could find. In one area of the home, evidence points to desperation as he had used horseshoe nails from fallen warhorses to repair cannonball-damaged flooring.

What's interesting is this house was once that of a showcase home. It was a place where Mr. Lotz could have customers over to see his carpentry work to choose which window frame or fireplace style they wanted. Beautiful woodwork that survived the battle is evidence that Mr. Lotz's attention to detail was valuable to him and his line of work. However, war aftermath work on the home points to the necessity to rebuild with only one goal, shelter. The family was left with the cleanup and heartache after battle occurred, a battle they did not participate in. Yet somehow, tragedy was exactly what led this family on a path toward purpose.

It took the family years to clean up the mess left behind. Once the work was done, Mr. Lotz made a piano with artwork on it that was reflective of the battle that had occurred. The KKK heard about the piano and was determined Mr. Lotz and his son would be tarred and feathered. Knowing the violence that was imminent, Mr. Lotz loaded his family into a wagon and traveled to California. While on the journey, Matilda Lotz, Mr. Lotz' daughter, saw a wolf and painted a painting of the animal. Matilda's painting was noticed, and this led her on the path to San Francisco School of Design. Matilda became a prominent artist who traveled all over the world, selling art for top prices.

What if she stayed in Franklin, Tennessee? What if the family never faced such hardships that forced them from their home? (What if Israelites never headed out to the promised land? What if you never chose to lay your captivities behind?)

Very few people actually deserve their trials, floods, storms, or battles. However, surviving heartache can lead a person directly to the path of their God-designed purpose. Pain is part of the journey. Does God see that others have needs for stories of triumph? Could it be that whatever you may be facing someone else needs? Could it be that the pages of Job comfort the hurting so they know they are not alone? Could it be that a person who needs bold faith could not find such from any other than Noah? Noah's story, Job's story, the Lotz family, and so many of these stories on the pages of history and biblical text are almost unbelievable. Is your story somewhat unbelievable, even to you?

Some say these stories aren't relevant anymore. But when a person is facing mountains of their own, when problems arise that leave one saying, "I couldn't make this stuff up," that is when bold faith is needed. It is when a person can't believe the enormity of their problems is real, that they need a story that says, "If Job can survive, so can I. If Noah did, so will I."

When you find yourself in the midst of a flood knowing you didn't deserve it, you may find that someone will later need your testimony. You may find slaves looking for the Promised Land on your path. Tell your story. Then they, too, can have bold faith that not only weathers the storms but also has the perseverance to clean up the aftermath of floods. Then and only then will they make it to their glory.

But making it through to the, "I survived," part of the story is hard. Some claim God never gives more than we can handle. If this were true, why would anyone need God? Most of us couldn't handle our storms without his help, but he does help. He does give directions. It is our obedience to those directions that determines the outcome.

When reading about the specs for the ark in Genesis 6:14, it could almost be overwhelming to read, maybe not even make sense to those who weren't made to build the ark. The details are a bit much—X cubits high, and Y cubits deep. However, if you were going to survive this particular type of flooding, you would want those details. God is in the details of survival. His details are overwhelming and occasionally confusing. (Let me clarify. God isn't the author of confusion but of perfect peace. But our minds and hearts can become confused on the road. That's why we need him.)

Furthermore, the details God gives to the one facing the trial don't always make sense to the outsider. (This is why you have to pack the willingness to look nuts into your overnight bags.) It's okay when others don't understand; they aren't the ones surviving the flood. But when you're Noah, blind obedience is important.

Floodwaters are overwhelming. It's also overwhelming to think God would ask more of us than we could ever do. Sometimes the hard reality of a flood is we can't do it. Imagine that God told you to gather two of every kind of animal. Where does one find so many animals? God didn't do that though. God never said, "Noah, go get two tigers, good luck catching them," while perched on a cloud laughing at Noah's clumsy attempts to capture the wild beast. God expected Noah to build a place for the animals and keep them, but God brought the animals to Noah. God will bring you to deep waters, but he will provide the instructions on how to build shelter. He is your shelter. God will do his part to complete his works. He will bring you into flowing waters.

Focus Scriptures

> Not only so, but we also glory in our sufferings, because we know that suffering produces perseverance; perseverance, character; and character, hope. (Romans 5:3–4 NIV)

Chapter 11

Uncharted Territory

I enjoy having breakfast by the lake. It is something I can do when I need solace and to recenter. I sit, read, pray, and watch. Most mornings, I watch retired men arrive boats in tow to enjoy their leisurely fishing.

Every time I watch, I somehow expect a different result. Gracefully they back their boats into the water. One man will dismount the boat and then pull the boat up to the dock, and their friend will jump in. I think I secretly watch waiting for the moment when the truck-driving mate takes it too far and plunges his truck into the water. Or I almost believe one day, one of these unsuspecting men will fall off the dock instead of making it into the boat. Maybe I expect these things to happen because I know if I were in either role, this is the exact sequence others would enjoy watching. I've yet to see these things. I usually just watch until the boats disappear into the fog.

However, I recently arrived at the boat dock and almost felt a little confused by the scenery. Not one fisherman. No fog. I was so used to the scenery that I almost felt like I was in a foreign land. Once I realized why everything looked so different, I settled into the idea of enjoying the "new" scenery.

I watched birds dancing on the lake, and I admired the architecture of beautiful castle like homes I actually never noticed before. When the boats did come, I enjoyed watching the rippled patterns the boats made. It wasn't that I hadn't seen these things before. It was that in this particular spot, I was very accustomed to the fog. A clear day seemed bizarre.

How did the Israelites feel when they finally made it away from "that one mountain"? They had been traveling around it for forty years. It probably became so comfortable to look at anything else would certainly feel unnatural.

Once you begin seeing flowing waters that carry you away from your wilderness, the new land will have discomfort associated with it. It doesn't mean you're off track, it only means you're not used to the new. If you've spent years in debt and only know living paycheck to paycheck, the feeling of not having bill-related anxiety may produce anxiety.

If you've only known bad relationships, having fulfilling relationships may leave you to expect the ball to drop at any moment. It may even cause you to force your partner to write spiritual checks for debts they never accrued. If you've spent years trying to achieve anything in particular, you may find it distractingly uncomfortable once you don't have to struggle.

When you recognize the scenery is different and you've finally arrived, it may be very hard to settle into your promised land. Settling into and becoming lazy are two different things that don't confuse the two.

A woman may marry and almost forget her life's purpose and become complacent to purpose. It's easy to forget what brought us to any point is that God wanted to use the battle for good. Couples will often become so comfortable they stop pursuing one another.

The promises of God are meant to give him glory. You still have to work, but God chose you to occupy this land for a reason. Even if you're a little uncomfortable even if the new seems like a foreign land, God placed you there with purpose. As God has shed many things off of you, has he began showing you ways he expects you to live in purpose, walk with purpose?

Almost There

I've often wondered why the Israelites traveled around the same mountain for forty years. Why didn't they climb that same mountain to gain a new directional perspective? Then I questioned if they did climb the mountain, would they settle at the top? It would make sense in some areas to stay. Would the elevation of that mountain be enough to pass the snake line? If so, wouldn't it make perfect sense for the Israelites to stay where there was no threat of snakes?

The snake line is often spoken about in Christian culture. It is said that snakes cannot survive above a certain elevation. So many pastors refer to higher living as living above the snake line. But how do you expect to get there? The only way to this higher elevation life-style is walking through areas where snakes exist. The reality? As you tread overhead, snakes won't like it and will likely attack.

Here you are, you've come so far, yet the attack is strong. Actually, the attack you may face now could be stronger than you have ever experienced. The closer you get, the worse your battle may be.

Haven't you considered the serpent hates your progress? Have you contemplated the attack that will come on the journey upward? Frequently, a person who is under attack will misunderstand the war-zone. They may believe it is due to wrongdoings or even being out of God's will. However, the opposite is usually more accurate. A person who is climbing higher toward their purpose will face unbelievable attack. Consider Jesus as he was alone and tempted by Satan as the serpent did not want his purpose to unfold.

Imagine that snake line now. Might I submit to you that you're close? You're coming to the higher elevations where serpents cannot exist. Satan wants to get all attacks in before he has to flee. Satan may strike at you. But you keep walking. The landscape may be unfamiliar; that's only because this is new ground. This doesn't mean you're out of God's will. It simply means Satan doesn't like your progress or your purpose.

Protected Purpose

When I was a small child, I was playing with a friend and went behind my parents' house. I was back there for a minute before I realized that I was standing just a few inches from a snake. It sat coiled up looking at me as if to say, "Aren't you going to run?" When I did see the snake, I did run in the house and tell my mom.

Mom called my grandfather, and he came to kill the snake. He told us it was a copperhead. The thing is, I was around this snake so unaware for longer than makes sense for it to not strike.

As you climb higher, remember, the attacks may seem real heavy. But just like that snake and my smaller being, without God's permission, serpents can never strike you. You may be feeling serious pressure and warfare. However, it's possible you're unaware of what attacks are created with your name in mind. Similar to the snake that I stood near for longer than makes sense without attack, you could be protected from more than you know.

You've Arrived

What if you heard those beautiful words from your GPS, "You've arrived at your destination"? If only the journey was that simple. Oh, if only. The simplicity. After forty excruciating years, would you plop your satchel down and fall to the ground for an exhausted nap? Would you take the time to breathe it all in? Really breathe in the scenery? Look around at what God has done. Look back over the path and all the changes that happened in you. Look at the beauty that lies before you.

Sometimes it's hard to know if the storm is even over. Is it safe to come out of the arc? Where's the dove carrying an olive branch to say, "It's okay to come out of the confined walls of your ship. The flood is gone." The lessons you've learned; they're part of your safety net. Those lessons have taught you more than you know. You've learned more about how not to repeat your strongholds. However, it will take some work on your behalf to walk in your promises. It will take more than belief to survive your promises. It will take passion, work, determination, persistence, and a protective coating of prayer.

Protective Prayer

While eating with a group of friends one evening, one of my homies (yes, I said homies) told a story about a doctor he does some work with. This friend reported that one of his clients informed him of a desire to change careers. The doctor (client) no longer had a passion for medicine like he once did. Instead, his heart was in… blueberries.

The beginning of the storyline alone points to the extreme opposites of purposes. God can be eccentric of this, I'm certain. If you are reluctant to agree, I'm willing to argue my stance. Virgin birth. Stuttering, murdering leader. Saul yielded Paul. Widowed bride. Orphaned Queen. Do I dare to continue? Why not? The author of the book you're reading was terrible in all things English and hated the class. I'm a country gal; English is a second language. Has my point become redundant?

God seems to dabble in the art of oxymoronic living. Your story may be similar in that it makes no real sense but by the grace of God and through his purpose. But it seems I've ventured from my point. Where was I? You don't know? Me either.

Oh yes, blueberries. This particular doctor took my friend to his blueberry farm to show him the intricacies of farming blueberries. My comrade is a bit of a math mind so what intrigued him was the sheer amount of water that it takes to protect a blueberry during freezing temperatures.

When cold weather threatens the fruit, a blueberry farmer will coat the berries in sequence. Farmers spray layers of water over the plants. They allow each layer to freeze and repeat. This continues until the plants are covered enough to be protected from harsh conditions.

My math-minded nerd of a friend did the calculations. What it all translates to is this particular farmer used the equivalent of one hundred and thirty-seven backyard pool's worth of water to protect his harvest.

Like the physician/farmer in this story, your former passion may have died. If so, it's okay. Seasons change. Similar to the MD, it may take a little side hustle to make the other passion reap any real harvest. You're going to need a lot more than what meets the eyes to fully walk in your purpose. Purpose requires work. Passion determination, and persistence is necessary.

Mostly, like the massive amounts of water that protect fruit, it is essential to saturate your purpose in protective layers of prayer... and lots of it.

Chapter 12

Purposely Promised

When God flooded the earth, it was as if he was taking a blemished canvas and repainting what he originally intended the earth to be. When a person goes through trials of any kind, God is often doing the same for that person. What's left does not look like what existed before the storm. Those previous trees and creatures that existed before the storm, well, what remains often seems like a mess. You may feel like what is left of you after your storm or wilderness looks like an entirely different being than what was before. And it is. But what we do with the mess is vital. How we allow God to repaint our canvas is crucial to living in the promises of God.

When the high waters of trouble entered into your life, it may be that God was cleansing your slate so that you can live in his intended purpose, "multiply" the Promised Land. So many take this command to multiply as though it means to have a multitude of children. If you're called to raise a baseball team, more power to you. But I'm convinced God is telling us, multiply his kingdom of believers, and he is giving us direct instructions on how to do so. He will ask us to bear the fruits ("be fruitful") of the spirit. (Love, joy, peace, patience, kindness, goodness, faithfulness, gentleness, and self-control.)

That sweet precious fruit, it is so delightful that few can refuse its taste. And when others taste of it, they come back for more. They learn who God is and want to be part of his kingdom. Once there, they too will learn their purposes and further multiply God's kingdom.

Make no mistake the fruits of the spirit are from him. If you're feeling tension in your neck considering your shortcomings, you're in good company. Many stress as they consider themselves and their shortcomings. That's because they're considering their fruit, not fruit of the spirit (John 15:5). The only way to bear this fruit is to stay rooted in Jesus. (Feeding on nutritional fruit from the Father, referring back to chapter 2.) Then seeds planted in others will arm them for their battles and journey toward God and his purpose for their lives.

Above all, Christians are accountable to raise armies for God's purposes. (Armies against Satan and his plans, not one another.) Are you showing others how beautiful and great God is? Are you using your survival purpose and talents as a chance to increase the kingdom? Are you going back to the slaves to help them make it to the Promised Land?

After Noah left the ark, God gave him instructions to "be fruitful and multiply." This instruction was given several times in the Bible. The first time the command was mentioned was to Adam and Eve. "Be fruitful and multiply." This was God's original plan for mankind. The Garden of Eden was his kingdom. God wanted it to be multiplied. He purposed Adam and Eve to tend to this garden and to expand what was already "good."

Through trials and floods, our Father begins showing us what his purpose for our life is. He will show (or has been showing) you glimpses of your purpose on the journey toward the Promised Land. Writing was the only release I felt in the early days of my wilderness seasons. I believed that if I was facing hardships, surely someone else was too. And maybe just maybe if I helped one person with my words, it was all worth the pain. I never enjoyed writing prior to having to face the reality of bearing my cross. Yet as I began sharing my words of encouragement, I found a lot of people needed those words. Has God been giving you constructive ways to relieve your pain? Have you found that painting helps you feel relief? Or have you found music to be cathartic during your journey? Have you found that the pain of your wilderness has given you a spirit of encouragement toward those who are facing the same trials?

Has lack and hunger shown you new compassion toward those who are living impoverished and unable to eat? Did your wilderness or enslaved life create a desire to start new charities or ministries? Sharing these talents in the spirit of love, goodness, gentleness, kindness, self-control…is part of being fruitful.

Being fruitful in our purpose is how we can take control of our pain. Being fruitful is to relieve our lives from Satan's grip. It is how we can keep our flooded marshlands from becoming wastelands. Being fruitful in purpose is how God gets the glory for the pain. It takes back the power of Satan's plan and restores God's divine schematics. Do not let Satan have the final say. If he wrecked your world, make him pay. Tell others about God so that they too can claim victory over hell's plan for their lives. Your life's testimony is of great value to the kingdom of God. Is it possible that after your flood, God is giving you the same command he gave to Noah? How will God call you to multiply his kingdom?

Survivalist Eyewitness Account

What would a thirty-minute conversation with Noah reveal? What questions would you have for him if you could have a short lunch with Noah?

Once someone survives a flood, they possess knowledge they didn't even know they lacked prior to their trial. Is it possible that someone who is facing the same trial you have faced would love to have a thirty-minute Q and A session with you?

Have you ever been around someone who could live in the wilderness off berries and ants alone? They possess fascinating knowledge about what is poisonous and what is good. They know how to listen to the winds of change to seek shelter. They know subtle signs that the ground we walk on is unsafe. They didn't learn about the ways of the land by wishing; they learned the way of the land by walking through and surviving it.

What wilderness did you survive? Do you know about what is safe specific to your wilderness and what is unsafe for a spirit to digest? Have you seen the shifting sands of financial wastelands fall out from under you? Do you now know what grounds are safe to stand on? Have you seen a shift in weathered relationships and know how to seek shelter with God? You friends were made to survive your specific wilderness but survive with purpose and operate in a gift from God. Someone needs your account. How has God been prompting you to operate in his purpose? Has he been showing you something about your talents that would benefit others? Has God been prompting you to witness? Has he shown you how your wounds could help others heal?

The Purpose of Hardship

When my father was younger, he struggled to read. His teachers sat him down to learn with what sounded like a machine that would only show one line at a time. Line by line, Dad became an excellent reader.

Years later, my dad was working as a mechanic. He was very good at what he did. And he was the one who always helped others with what he knew. In his work, he met a man who couldn't read very well. When the man didn't know how to do a particular job, Dad would go to the man's area and read the instructions to him.

One evening, the man apologized for not knowing how to read. He was embarrassed by this. Dad told him he was happy to help him learn. So together, they began to sound out words. It began with the man not fully understanding what he had read, but he was reading.

Eventually, Dad's cohort became excited about reading. He came to work and proudly told my dad how he had signed up for a high school class to help him read.

Had my father not struggled in his early years, would he have been sympathetic to his coworker's needs? Maybe. But his knowledge of how it felt to struggle likely made it easier to be patient, understanding, and kind to a soul in need. This is only a small sample of how our lives can be used. When we survive storms, we then have responsibilities that follow. And what a great joy that is to be a part of.

Emancipation Proclamation

During the American civil war, most African Americans weren't allowed to fight in the war. This all changed with the Emancipation Proclamation. The first regiment of Black soldiers was formed creating the Fifty-Fourth Massachusetts Volunteer Infantry Regiment. It only made sense that former slaves would have strong interest in freeing their fellow man. One would be hard pressed to find anyone with a heavier burden toward the freedom of slaves.

How could a former drug addict become free from their addiction yet turn their backs on the prompting to war against drugs? Homeless persons who overcome poverty should have the greatest compassion toward others who suffer. A broken person who learns their identity should most definitely carry vested interest in freeing others.

There is no one with more intense regard to the strongholds of slavery than former slaves. You have been given an emancipation proclamation with permission to save others from the strife you've faced. Just as Ester became a queen for "such a time as this" to save her people, God placed you where you are to save your people. As Moses was offended by the mistreatment of his people, are you concerned by the strongholds over your spiritual people? Will you fight for your brothers and sisters?

It's a Romans 10:17 Kind of Life

Faith comes by hearing. Our stories are not our own to selfishly hold onto. Survival tales never told are only hardships that go in vain. Who could benefit from you not telling your story? Remember the rich man in the Bible? He stored up his riches in silos, unwilling to share. How sad. Your testimonials, your talents, and your gifts are your riches. Don't store them up unwilling to give others what you know. Just as unused perishable food stored away will rot, your testimonies that are never shared will wither and fade. But sharing keeps the works of God alive and gives others hope.

Once you've made it to the Promised Land, you have one job, witness, and rescue. Even when being a witness makes you uncomfortable, you have responsibilities to save other slaves. God didn't bring you this far for your selfish purposes.

It's understandable that it is uncomfortable to operate in your purpose. You may feel as uncomfortable as a vegetarian in a BBQ dive bar when it comes to sharing your faith. We never know how others may receive it.

It's often asked, "If a tree falls in the woods, does it make noise?" The answer is said to be "no" sound needs a receptive body to be heard. Naturally, many fear falling in the wilderness and then insult to injury, never being heard. Let this guide your prayers that your witness will fall on receptive ears.

It's also uncomfortable to witness because Christian life is sometimes like mosquito repellent to non-Christians. And it hurts to know that our love for God and desire to help others may push some away. We want to keep people in our lives. If you struggle with this, it may help to refer back to what stumbling blocks existed on your journey. Fear of losing someone is a stumbling block. What if in contrast to your feared result, you gain their affections on a deeper level?

If you're struggling with the stumbling block of your comfort zone, let me illustrate some examples of leaving others in the dark and alone in this cold world. Perhaps these illustrations will help you to gain the courage to lead others in love.

Alone

On an early October morning, I found myself going about business as usual. Working as a nurse meant I had to leave my house before 5:00 a.m. to drop my child off with my parents. He was six years old, facing the standard separation anxieties most young lasses would. Most mornings, I would wake my mom up and make my way out of the door. However, this particular morning, I laid my son down thinking that he would go back to sleep, and I locked the door behind me. As I made my way off, I felt some discomfort with leaving. So I turned around and started back. That's when I saw my son had followed me out. There he stood innocently, smiling his toothless grin, bright eyes shining, and offering a quiet, "Bye, Mom, I love you."

I smiled, hugged him, and said, "Go get in bed with Mamaw." But something told me to check the door. He had locked himself out. This particular morning was a crisp thirty-four degrees out. He was still in pajamas and had no coat, shoes, or socks on. What if I had not listened to that unsettling feeling to go back? A small child would have been locked out in the cold unprotected from the elements.

It would be hours before my parents woke up and noticed he wasn't there. I spent a large majority of the day feeling sick from the scenarios I played through in my mind. To say it left me unsettled is an understatement.

In reading, many could chastise my parental abilities. Most would be afraid to share this fumbled moment in parenting. But I want you to understand the true seriousness involved with a small child, unprotected in this world. Christians are called to more than ourselves. We have duties to bring others into the warmth of God. How is it so many are left out in the cold world of Satan's design? If the imagery of a small frozen babe isn't enough, perhaps I could illustrate the importance of witnessing and loving others with your particular gifts and the consequences of negligence on a deeper level.

In 1900, Galveston, Texas, experienced a nightmare like no other. The bustling town was hit by the most deadly hurricane in United States history. This single hurricane was the United States greatest natural disaster. But the worst part of the hurricane's devastation is that it was a direct result of egotistical and political negligence. This was no matter of ignorance but instead a matter of jealousy and pride that led to the loss of thousands of innocent lives.

The weather bureau's director was jealous of Cuban technology, so he shut down weather communications between Cuba and the US. Furthermore, Willis Moore (the bureau's director) made it known to US forecasters that they could not issue hurricane warnings without first going through Washington, DC. Therefore, hurricane warnings never made it to those who depended on responsible parties to advise them of impending doom. Due to Galveston residents' lack of knowledge regarding impending hurricane landfall, evacuation didn't occur. As a direct result of the negligence of the weather bureau, thousands perished.

What is it that you know or have learned as a result of your travels on the wilderness journey? Why did God choose to let you survive? Your trial was never your own. To journey the lonely and difficult path to a promised land and never share your testimony is a form of negligence. Why do you have information if you will not share? Is it pride? Do you fear rejection? What could the information you possess do for others?

Consider the cost. Consider those who helped you out of the wilderness. What if they chose not to do so? Consider the moments that had you enslaved. Remember the pain. You have mapped out a journey. You now know how to get to the Promised Land. If not, now you will.

Will you allow lives to perish because you're unwilling to share the most vital information you've learned with others? Not all would have fled from the hurricane of 1900 had they known. We know this behavior to be true with modern-day science and seeing that some chose to stay in harm's way. I have a friend whose father sat in his transfer truck as his mobile home was destroyed by a hurricane. It's doubtful he expected such severe weather.

You do not have to carry the burden of receptivity. That's God's to carry. For instance, if you have survived abuse and left a relationship, you know how to do so. When you see a woman who is in such a relationship, you may feel prompted to help her recognize the abuse. When she isn't receptive, it isn't your role to force your knowledge on her. It is your job to love her and follow God's direction for loving her. In his time and way, he will help her know when to let go. Then you may be the one he expects to help her do so safely.

I have stood in my kitchen, tugging on what I saw as a dead leaf on one of my plants. The leaf was just not coming off without a fight. I left the leaf with the thought that when the leaf fully dies the plant will eventually let it go.

Some folks are like the plant, they will hold on to what is dying, knowing full well that it won't last. All the while, that doesn't change their hope that they may nourish that small part back. It isn't our job to decide what people hold onto or where they place their hope. It isn't our job to force evacuation on those who refuse to leave dangerous situations. But it is our purpose to share our spiritual gifts with others. God does expect his gardeners to sow seeds. What growth occurs will only be revealed in his time.

Even if you cannot save all, to save just one life from struggles they don't otherwise have to face is victory. How has God called you to serve?

Who Am I?

Sitting across the table from my niece, I inquired, "What will you do when you're grown?" I love this question and hate it all at once. To ask the question gives children some idea they should know at a young age what their purpose is in life. However, to ask often offers very entertaining results, so I rarely can resist.

"A scientist." I'll admit I didn't expect that one. She was around seven, maybe eight years old, so I expected an answer like most small children would give. My daughter wanted to be a train engineer at Dollywood. My youngest son, a YouTuber, middle child, a ninja. Perhaps her answer in comparison to my children's was reflective of parenting styles. My face is red. But all the same, I was very impressed and excited.

"What makes you want to be a scientist?" I probed.

"Science is my favorite class. Did you know there are rocks in the desert that move?"

Her eyes lit up as she explained her interest and the phenomenon of boulders sliding through Death Valley.

"Interesting, how do you think they move? Do you think animals drive them? Or are they the ones moving them?"

"No, it ain't, Mimi." She giggled. "I don't know how they move, but I want to be a scientist so I can study things like that."

Okay, who invited the adult to dinner? So we consulted the Google machine and found our answers. When we were done, I was able to grow up a little and encourage her dreams, knowing that it's because of scientists we were able to find the answers. And sadly it's because of a scientist, I couldn't convince her animals had moved the rocks.

Why do large rocks move without a trace of evidence other than the trails they leave behind? It's a series of events, but we will sum it up with ice, wind, and climate change. The easier it is to understand the better. My third-grade mind wants it to be animals, and my disappointment is writing this. So there. Sigh.

It is an interesting phenomenon no doubt, but what occurs is actually somewhat simple. Ice forms during very specific desert climate changes, rocks that are sitting on the ice slide very slowly. Then the wind pushes the rocks, and the sun melts thin sheets of ice under the boulders.

What exactly does icy rock have to do with your walk? If a thin sheet of ice paired with wind can cause boulders to move, certainly you can move mountains. If a small child can spark the interest of a grown woman and shatter her animal mischief dreams all in one sentence, you can change small parts of this world too.

Moreover, as the ice melted away and left scientists baffled for so many years, your walk may baffle others. Your work may only ever be seen without a trace of your existence ever being known. Encouraging others into creating movement though, that is an incredible feat.

This is what is so valuable about a walk with God and loving others. When our lives touch them, there may be very little evidence of what occurred, but change is visible and incredible. You may be the wind that pushes boulders to new destinations.

Masterfully Used

A paintbrush, with the correct vision and in the right hands, can be a magic wand. My grandfather used to talk about how he couldn't understand how someone could create a picture from nothing.

"She just stood there painting, and she would say, 'Oh, it needs this, and it needs that,' all the while creating something I had no idea existed." These are the words my grandfather used to describe how enchanted he was by witnessing someone's artwork progression.

My grandfather was affected by artwork in ways the artist likely never knew or would even understand. After all, the strokes of their brush certainly felt as natural as breathing.

Have you ever looked at the walls of a museum and found yourself drifting to another world? Have you heard someone's story that affected you deeply? Hard to believe that there is something in you that could have that same effect on another, I know. But you have something.

Music to my heart is much like art to my papaw's eyes. I am amazed. I listen and wonder, *How did they think of this? How did the musician create such work?* There are songs that last so long with bizarre twists and turns. Regardless of how many times I hear these particular songs, I never tire of them. There is music I can hear that takes me to another world and some songs minister to my spirit in ways I could never describe.

I'm amazed by how some creations are so inspirational, yet the person who wrote them never knew of my existence. The composers only followed their hearts to create. As musicians lay their hearts out for other's ears, each note finds its way home to the bits of our souls that need them most.

To say I appreciate the works of a musician's hands is putting it lightly. I'm, simply put, fascinated. Music is truly a gift, and any soul who chooses to share that gift shares the most delightful experience with others. To be gifted is one thing. To share a gift is to give others something in ways their hearts could never repay.

With such an appreciation for the magic that occurs in the hands of a musician, I recently found my heart in a saddened state. I had taken a trip to our sweet American castle, the Biltmore Estate. I have been there a few times before, and each time, I noticed something different. I love the artwork that adorns the entire estate. The floral arrangements are incredible. The history and hospitality is astounding. The list of things to appreciate about this home, well, I could write an entire book on the subject alone.

However, this time, it was the sheer volume of instruments that grabbed my attention. There are pianos in places most would never conceive. Seriously, there is a piano near the bowling alley. It seemed out of place for one who thinks like me. But then again, who really thinks of putting a bowling alley in their home? I suspect my perplexed feelings were reflective of my small visions.

The dining hall has enormous organ pipes larger than my vocabulary could express. I observed, and my mind wandered, *I wonder how many of these pianos are in tune? Is the organ still working? What would it cost to tune the organ alone better yet the entire estate's worth of pianos.* And lastly, *it seems so sad to have all these instruments left idle without the stroke of talented hands embracing these keys.*

However beautiful any instrument is, an idle instrument is only a piece of furniture with no real purpose. You are no different. God created you with unique talents, desires, hopes, and dreams. He carefully designed you with purpose in mind. Like the hands that create masterpiece instruments, God worked diligently in creating you to be something that would affect others.

A person who does not live purposely and intentionally is the same as an idle instrument. Idle lives are like paintbrushes that never grace the presence of any canvas. Stagnant hands are that of an unused typewriter shelved in an author's home. All have potential, but none are effective. Idle instruments are like faith without works, dead.

Uncomfortable

Remember the stumbling block of "comfort zones?" Comfort zones are enemies of purpose. We've established that. But what about the uncomfortable zones of witness that is the Promised Land?

Once you're free from former strongholds, it is challenging to know how to act. Let's take a moment to acknowledge that. Even if you have all the wilderness lessons written on the tablets of your heart, the Promised Land is a new stomping ground with new rules and responsibilities.

I once heard TD Jakes describe the trouble and oppression that many African Americans experience in relation to the history of slavery. He was relating money strife that many have to the fact that slaves weren't paid for their services. Therefore, they didn't know how to manage money in a world that is ran by money. Many are playing a hard game of catch-up. Many have operated on a deficit and are having to learn how to walk in their purposes and only praying not to stumble.

If this is you, you're not alone. If you're uncomfortable in the Promised Land, that's understandable. You're in good company. Remember Ester? She was an orphan turned queen. David? Shepherd turned king. Ruth? Widow turned bride. I doubt any of our biblical greats felt comfortable with their calling at first. Most royals have the opportunity to grow and learn their way into their crown. Though that is the purpose of wilderness lessons, it still is hard to walk in purpose.

What about you? You, a former slave turned into king or queen with a purpose. Stop considering "you" and remember to consider God. And consider that like Moses was chosen to save his people because something in him found offense with mistreatment of Hebrews. God knows your ability to see offense with wrongdoing, strongholds, etc. He has also seen something in you he wants to use to save others.

Somehow, I believe I have managed to digress, or have I? Ramble, ramble, ramble, and back to discomfort. Many physicians, nurses, respiratory therapists, nurse assistants, etc. all can attest that the first time they experienced a true emergency their hearts flipped a little. They likely first considered themselves and questioned their decision-making abilities.

Walking into an emergent situation for the first time is uncomfortable to say the least, but more accurately speaking, it's scary or downright terrifying. "What if my decision leads to death?" "What was it I'm supposed to do first?" "Are my chest compressions deep enough? Fast enough?" "I bet these others think I'm incompetent."

On the flip side of this, those who have done "codes" a few times will report a new comfort with them. Some actually thrive in these moments. Odd as it may be, some enjoy them. It isn't that they want anyone to perish, but some are really good at making quick decisions, having fast reactions, and feel deep satisfaction when they see good outcomes from dire situations.

How did they get so good at handling these codes? By doing them. By applying what they learned in books to what they've seen historically and using it for the good in each situation. Healthcare and emergency personnel of all flavors have "been there, done that." They're savage beasts that no forces of health attacks want to reckon with. Because employees of these services refuse to let others perish without a fight. What it all boils down to is that they have a knowledge and refuse to let their wisdom stand idle.

What did you learn in your wilderness? Without your wilderness season knowledge, you have little to offer. Just as an everyday citizen has little to offer any patient outside of calling 911.

Take a second to thank God for your lessons. You now have something to apply to saving others. How have struggles shaped your talents? Are you willing to run to the "codes" (dire situations surrounding you) to save the lives of those who will otherwise perish? Are you willing to be uncomfortable for a moment to become strongly skilled in saving lives?

It's time to operate in the power and beauty of your Promised Land purpose. So as I would say to any novice nurse, afraid to touch patients, standing against the walls, "Get in there, kiddo. The only way to learn this is by walking it. They will perish from your hesitancy. You're going to save lives."

Welcome to the Promised Land.

Key Focus Scriptures

I am the vine; you are the branches. If you remain in me and I in you, you will bear much fruit; apart from me, you can do nothing. If you do not remain in me, you are like a branch that is thrown away and withers; such branches are picked up and thrown into the fire and burned.

If you remain in me and my words remain in you, ask whatever you wish, and it will be done for you. (John 15:5)

But the fruit of the spirit is love, joy, peace, patience, kindness, goodness, faithfulness, gentleness, and self-control, against such things there is no law. (Galatians 5:22–23)

Consequently, faith comes by hearing the message, and the message is heard through the word about Christ. (Romans 10:17)

But you will receive power when the Holy Spirit has come upon you; and you shall be my witnesses both in Jerusalem, and in all Judea and Samaria, and even to the remotest part of the earth. (Acts 1:8)

But if the watchman sees the sword coming and does not blow the trumpet to warn the people and the sword comes and takes someone's life, that person's life will be taken because of their sin, but I will hold the watchman accountable for their blood. (Ezekiel 33:6)

From everyone who has been given much, much will be demanded: and from the one who has been entrusted with much, much more will be demanded. (Luke 12:48)

What good is it, my brothers and sisters, if someone claims to have faith but has no deeds? Can such faith save them? Suppose a brother or a sister is without clothes and daily food. If one of you says to them, "Go in peace; keep warm and well fed," but does nothing about their physical needs, what good is it? In the same way, faith by itself, if it is not accompanied by action, is dead. (James 2:14–22 NIV)

Do not oppress a foreigner; you yourselves know how it feels to be foreigners, because you were foreigners in Egypt. (Exodus 23:9 NIV)

Afterword

Standing at the crossroads, I felt pressure to get it right. I must choose a path that would financially secure my children's future, witness to others, and I should enjoy the fruits of my labor as well, right? I had worked for years as a nurse and was tired of my position. I felt prompting for change, but how? I had a few choices: (1) go back to school and further my career as a nurse practitioner, (2) school for architecture sounded more pleasing, and finally, (3) start taking writing a little more seriously.

I just wasn't sure which path God would want from me. So I decided to sign up for school for continued nursing, and if this was my path, school would happen, right? I had friends who offered to go with me! I was quickly accepted into all the schools I applied for! But my heart wasn't sure. Maybe architecture? Similarly, doors opened. I began meeting architects, and they all encouraged me to chase that dream. As for writing? I met more authors than I have ever met in my life, and they all supported the desire to publish, as did longtime friends and family members. A lot of those happenstance meetings with authors led to me receiving a lot of gifted books from them. Now what? It seemed God could be invested in all of these paths.

I prayed, and then I had a dream. I was hiking when I arrived at a three-pathed crossroad. Cross path? Whatever, there I stood confused and uncertain. Where should I go? I could see the end of no path. The first path on the right sparked no interest. (Deep down, I believe this was representative of my heart toward furthered nursing.) The path to the left, it was pretty but not very intriguing. The third pathway looked beautiful but a little extreme. (You can guess this is what I felt represented my writing endeavors.)

Still, I was unsure which way to go. That's when I heard God say, "Look up. Keep your eyes on me, and I'll show you where you belong. But wherever you go, I am with you."

That's when I knew God wouldn't make any decisions for me. I didn't like that bit of knowledge at the time. I was hoping he would allow me to passively seek his guidance. And he would show me where to go. In hindsight, I'm thankful God doesn't force us to take any paths. That's slavery.

I had a deep burning in me, and I knew I must take a path toward writing. It was like that center path of my subconscious, extreme looking somewhat scary but beautiful. Likewise, it would require grunt work, but mostly faith to make it. Writing seemed to be a bit of a gamble. Writing is a faith journey with no guarantees, but I knew God would go with me. My job? Look up and keep my eyes on him.

It hasn't been easy; the lessons on these pages came from many tears. As God had to teach them to me so I could put them to paper. Be assured that any tears you've battled through these pages, I was behind the pages with a bleeding heart and prayers for my promises to write the words. As I wrote, I prayed each word would find the hearts who needed them most.

I have battled with every wilderness-Promised Land obstacle, all the way down to not having anything but my cell phone to write with. That's right. More than the majority of this book was written with my two thumbs, but God still made it happen. He was still with me.

As I'm working on the finality of this book, my friends are finishing their journeys to furthered nursing careers. I'm so proud of them. But my heart is at peace. I know I took the road that was laid out for me. I know the struggles were worth the outcome. I know that the bloodied noses I've experienced on my journey are what opened the door to who I am.

I've found the only path in life worth taking is the one that seems a little harder. After hiking and taking harder trails time and time again, I've found many short easy paths offer little reward. Life is no different. Sometimes we have to make choices that will take hard efforts, and the only way we can stand on the promise is through our faith and faith alone. But the walk with our father is worth it.

This is what I hope to spark in all my readers, a flame in their hearts that refuses to take the easy path. And I pray all my readers know God will be on the journey with you. I hope that the only journey you will ever be satisfied with is that of which requires faith to achieve. The journey that can be accomplished with you and you alone, is that really worth traveling? Take the road that can only be achieved by the grace of God. That's the journey worth traveling.

Love,
M. L. Johnston

References

"Biography of Nelson Mandela." Nelson Mandela Foundation, October 29, 2014. www.nelsonmandela.org/content/page/biography.

Budanovic, Nikola. 2018. "The Origin of the Phrase 'Drunk as Cooter Brown' Dates Back from the American Civil War and Refers to a Heavy Drinker Who Escaped Being Drafted Due to His Continuous Intoxication." War History Online. Accessed July 22, 2019. www.history/phrase-drunk-as-cooter-brown.html.

Cohen, Patricia. "The Story Behind 'Woman in Gold': Nazi Art Thieves and One Painting's Return." *The New York Times*, March 30, 2015. www.nytimes.com/2015/03/31/arts/design/the-story-behind-woman-in-gold-nazi-art-thieves-and-one-paintings-return.html.

Davis, Paul. "Counterfeit Money: How to Spot Fake Bills." How Business Know How, September 30, 2019. www.businessknowhow.com/security/counterfeitmoney.html.

Greenfield, Amy Butler. *A Perfect Red: Empire, Espionage and the Quest for the Colour of Desire*. Black Swan, 2011.

History.com Editors. Updated April 14, 2010. The 54th Massachusetts Infantry. Retrieved September 21, 2020. https://www.history.com/topics/american-civil-war/the-54th-massachusetts-infantry.

"Il Diritto Di Contare = (Hidden Figures)." Twentieth Century Fox Home Entertainment, 2017.

International, Survival. "Sentinelese." Sentinelese—Survival International, www.survivalinternational.org/tribes/sentinelese.

Little, B. Posted August 29, 2017. "How the Galveston Hurricane of 1900 Became the Deadliest US Natural Disaster." Retrieved September 21, 2020. https://www.history.com/news/how-the-galveston-hurricane-of-1900-became-the-deadliest-u-s-natural-disaster.

Mims, Bryan. "Asheville's Fortress of Art: The Biltmore Estate." *Our State Magazine*, January 22, 2016. www.ourstate.com/biltmore-estate-art/.

Mullen, Luba. "How Trees Survive and Thrive After A Fire." National Forest Foundation, 2017. www.nationalforests.org/our-forests/your-national-forests-magazine/how-trees-survive-and-thrive-after-a-fire.

Paul Christian, Protect All Wildlife. "The Barbaric Tradition of 'Breaking the Spirit' of Elephants for Their Use in the Tourism Industry." One Green Planet, One Green Planet, February 4, 2015. www.onegreenplanet.org/animalsandnature/breaking-the-spirit-of-elephants-for-use-in-the-tourism-industry/.

"Radical Abolitionist *Par 5–6*." American Battlefield Trust. Accessed July 22, 2019. www.battlefields.org/learn/Ibiographies/john-brown.

Rettner, Rachael. "Teen's Junk Food Diet Caused Him to Go Blind, Doctors Say." LiveScience, Purch, September 7, 2019. www.livescience.com/teen-fussy-eater-vision-loss.html.

About the Author

If you don't know about M. L. Johnston, don't worry. No one else does either. That's because she lives a pretty mundane life in the foothills of Appalachia, Tennessee.

Messy house, messy mind, messy hair, and messy life. Seriously, the lady is a train wreck who uses her disastrous life lessons to help her readers get their lives together. She learns things the hard way so that you don't have to.

Johnston is a nurse by trade, mom by (happy) accident, and she uses painting and writing to escape it all. M. L. Johnston is determined to savor life and all it has to offer. Johnston enjoys hiking, biking, and random unplanned travel. Johnston is really good at starting DIY home renovations but not so great at completing them or much of anything for that matter. Yet somehow, she managed to complete this book using only a cell phone. This fact is one of the many reasons M. L. Johnston believes in miracles.